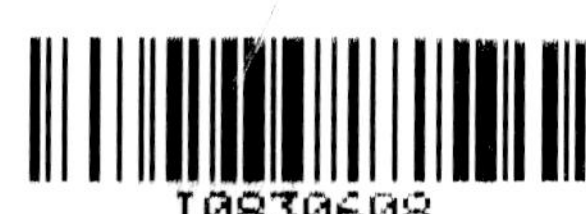

Animal
Coloring Book
FOR KIDS

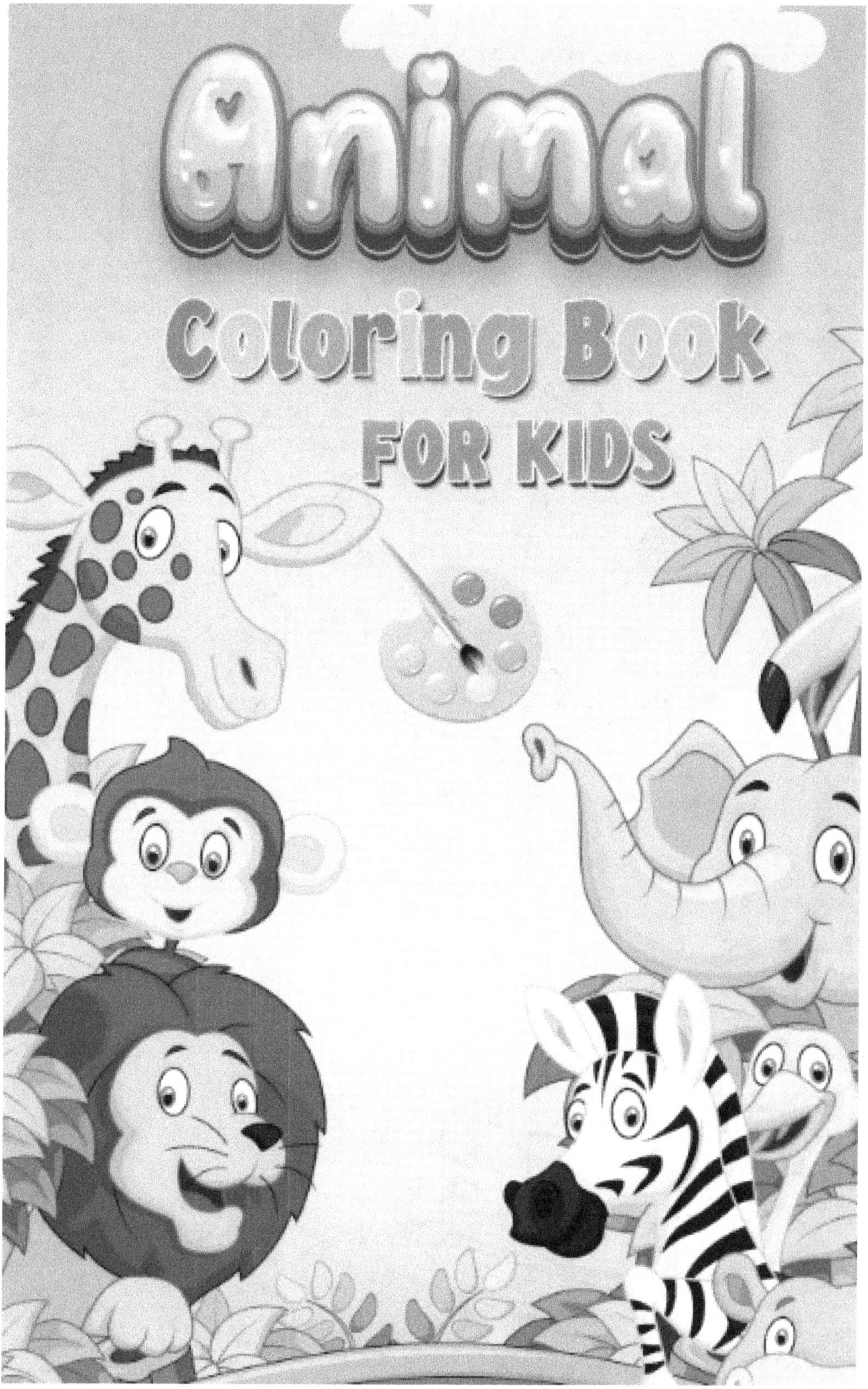

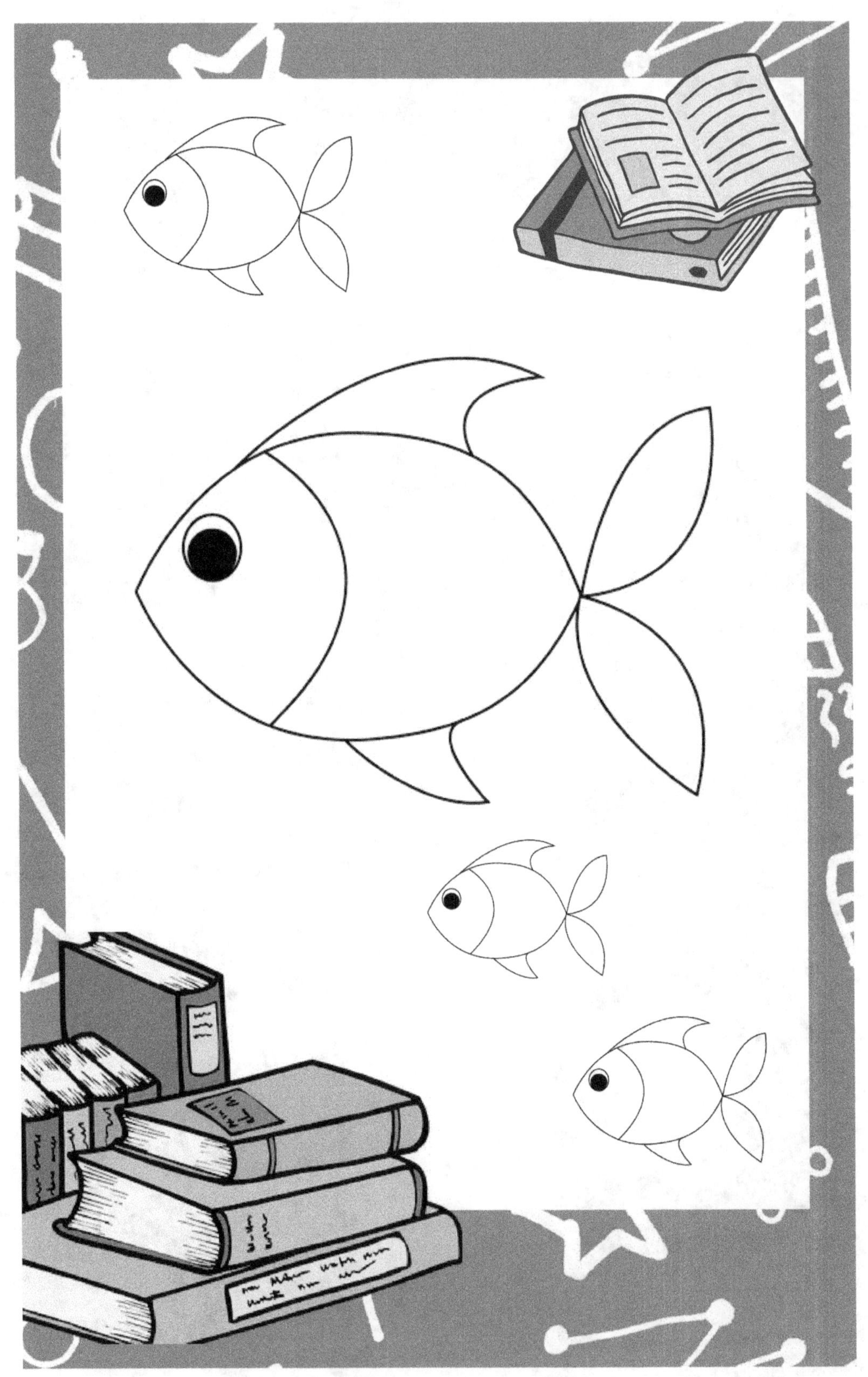

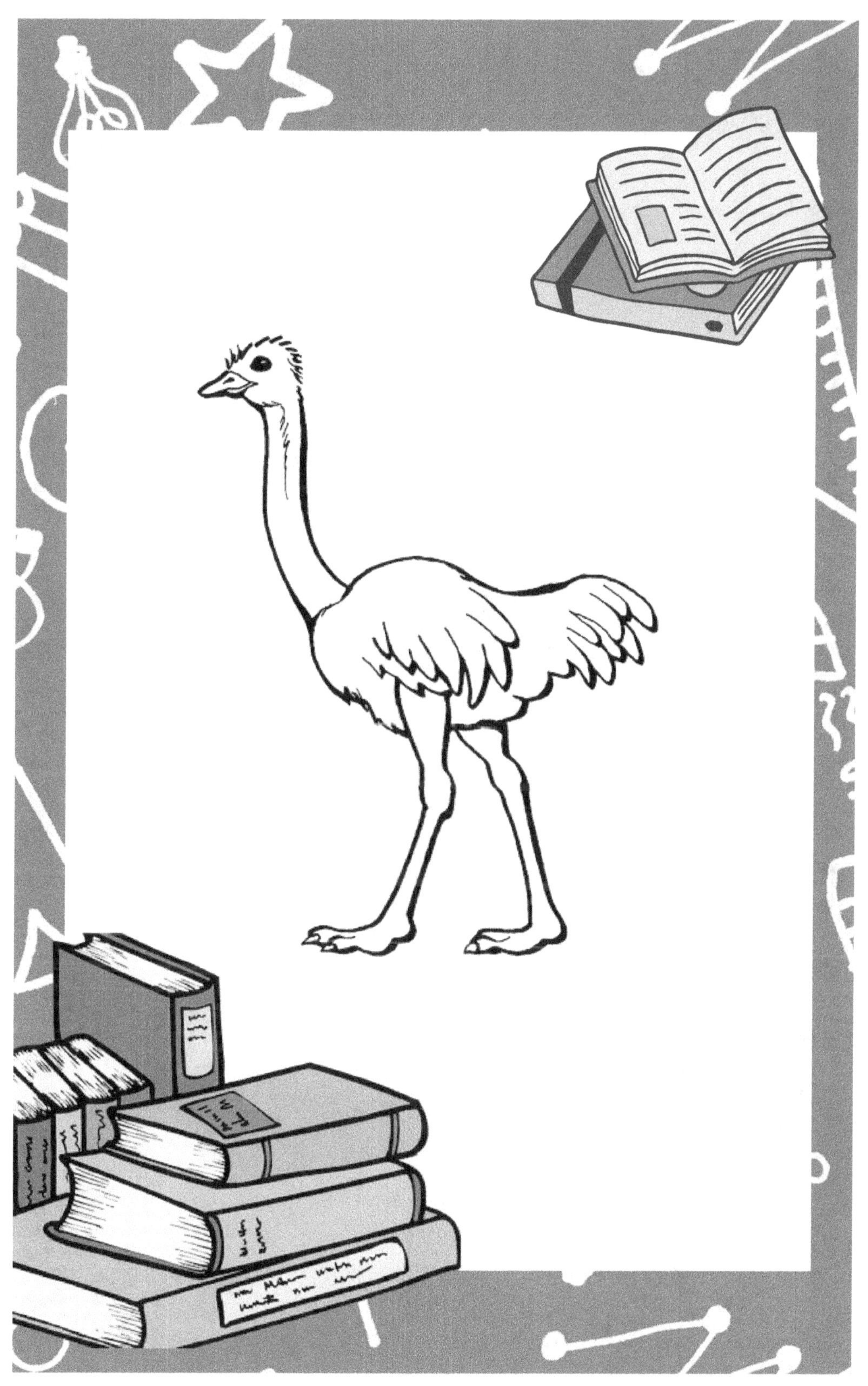

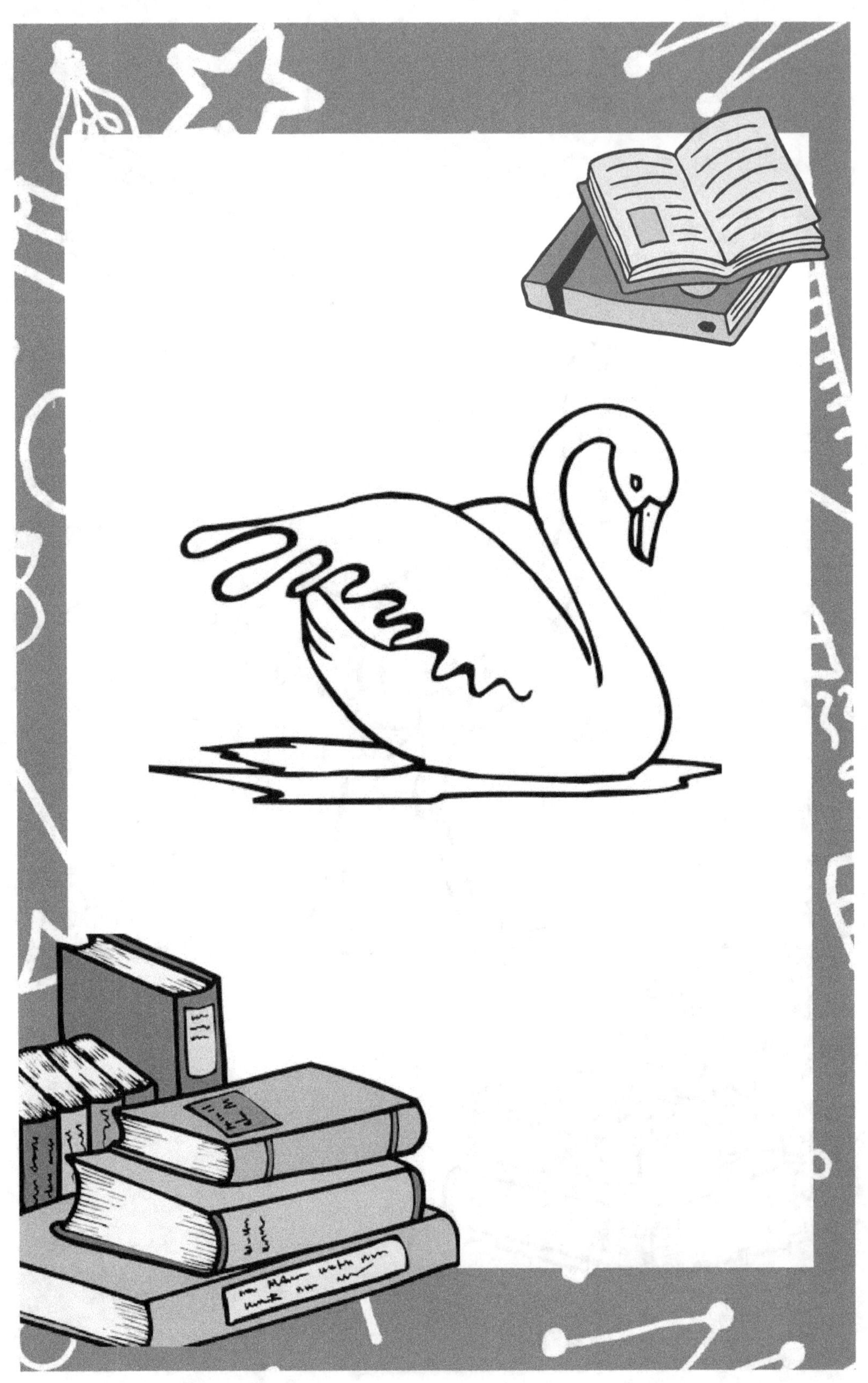

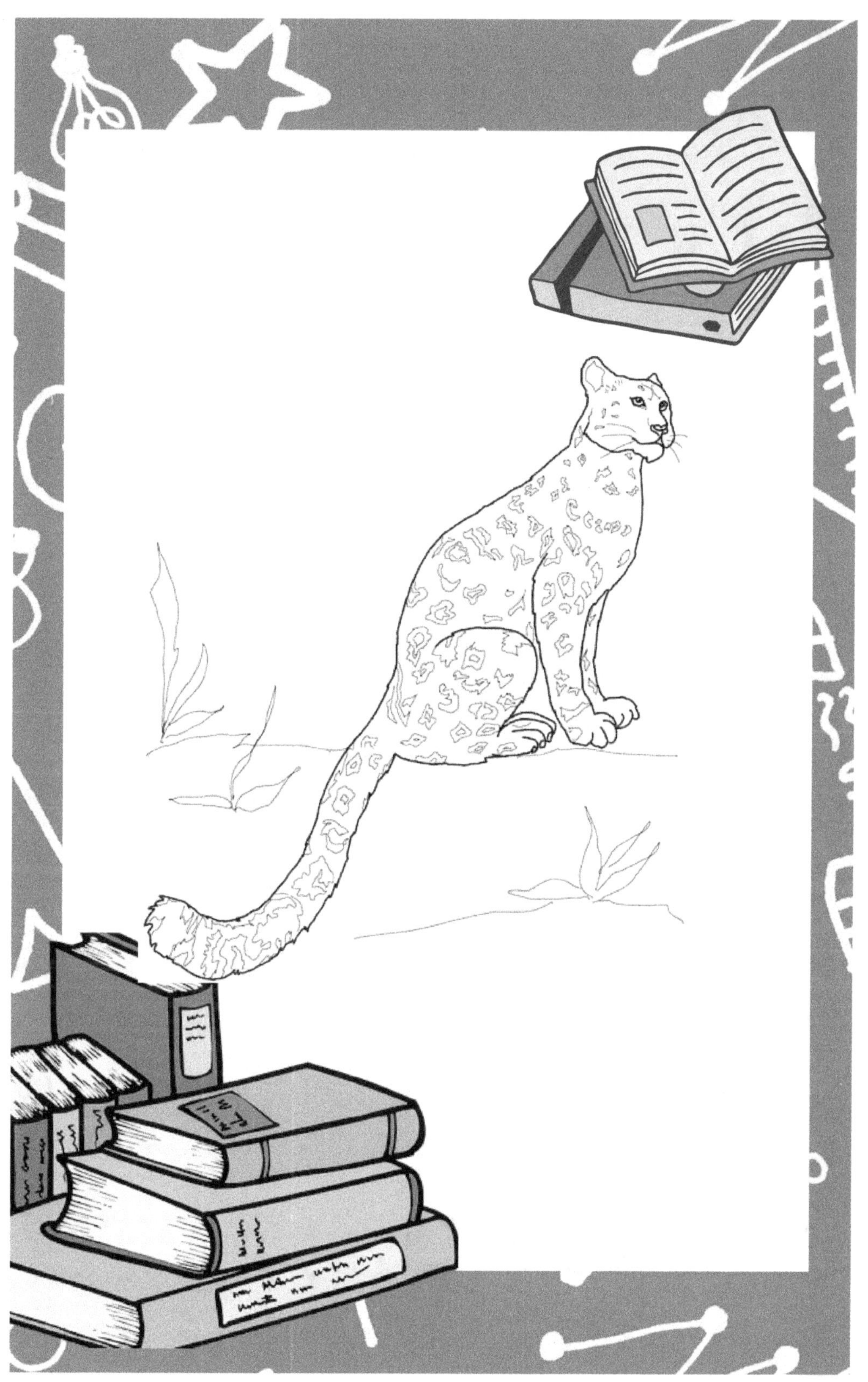

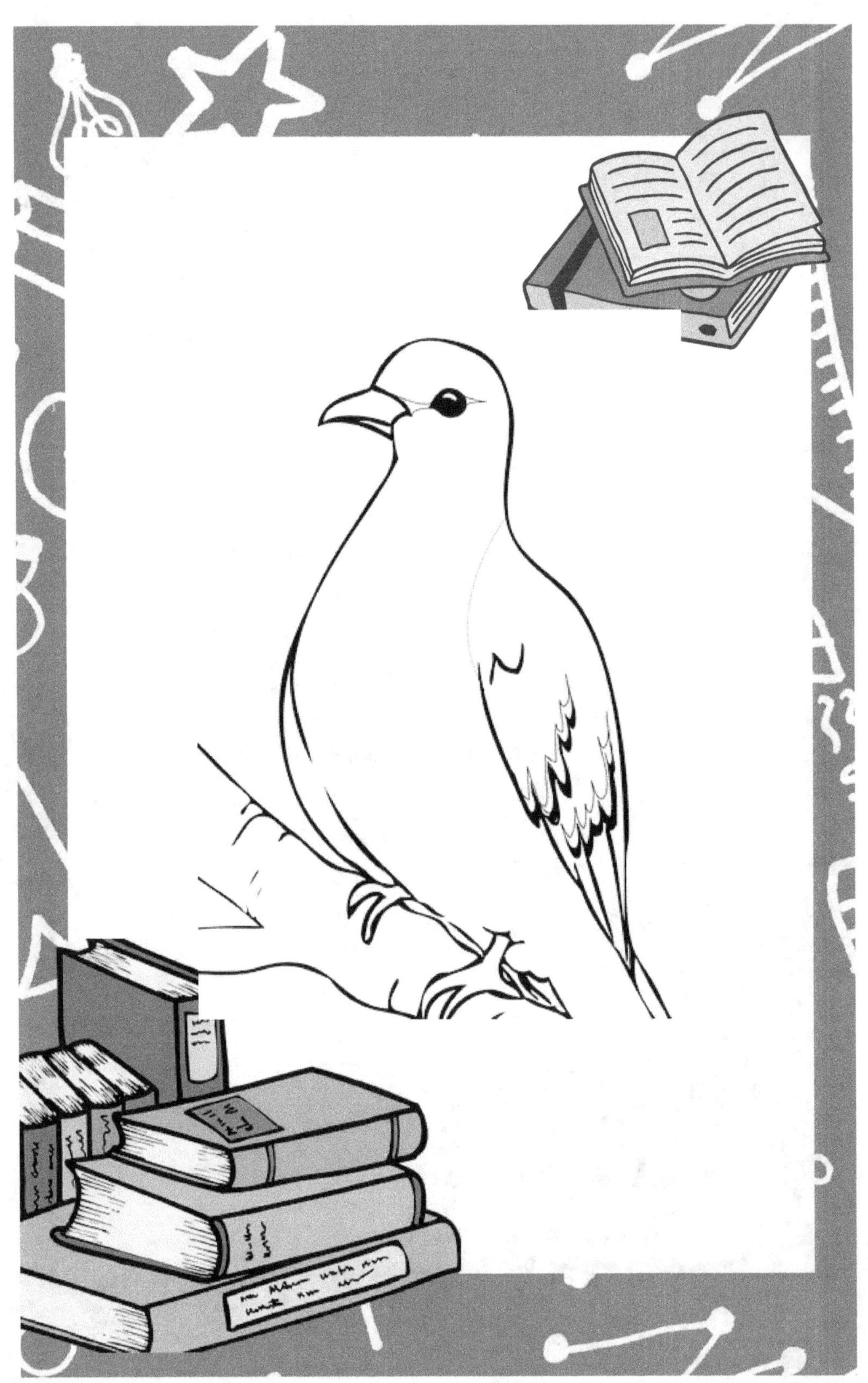

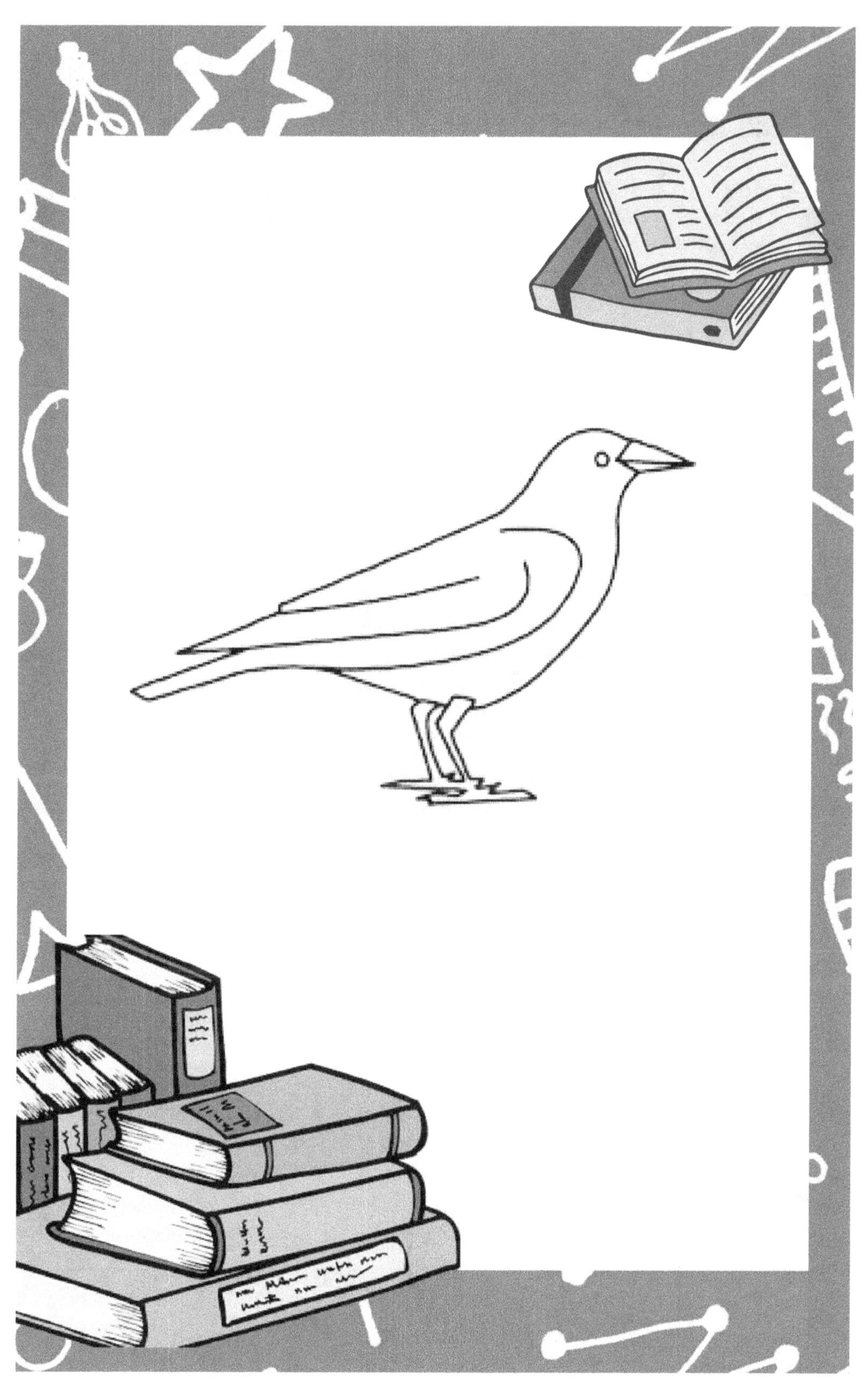

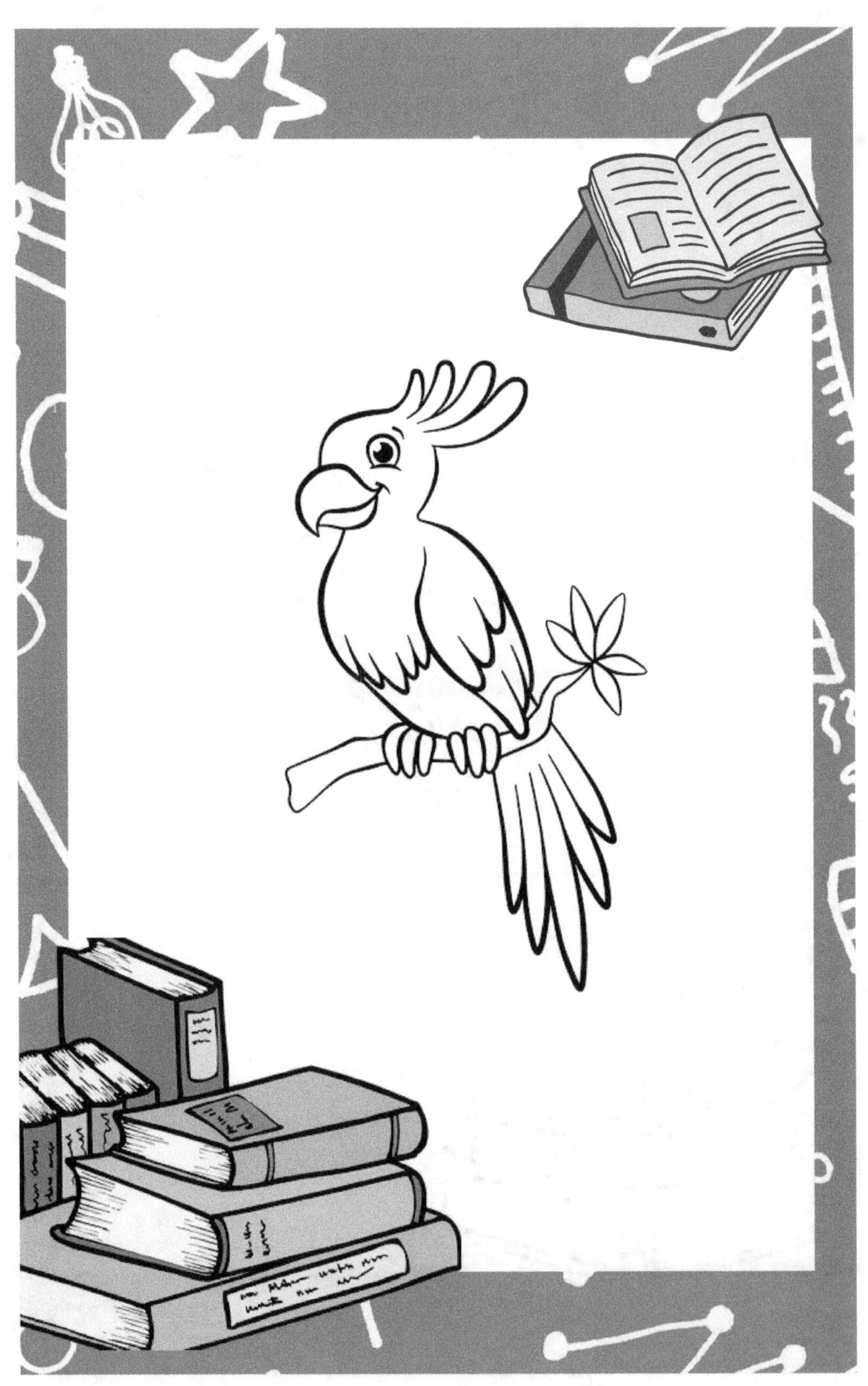

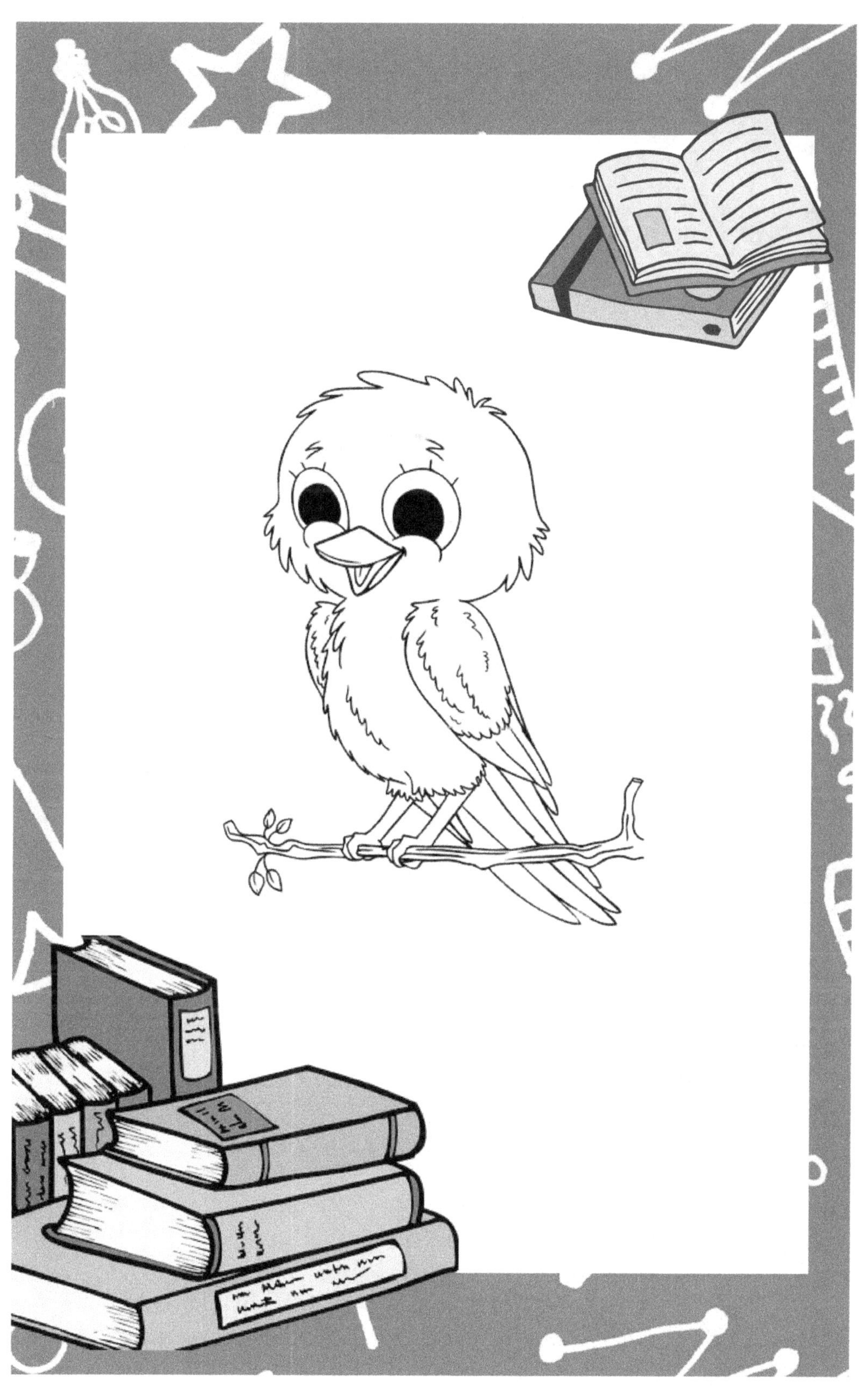

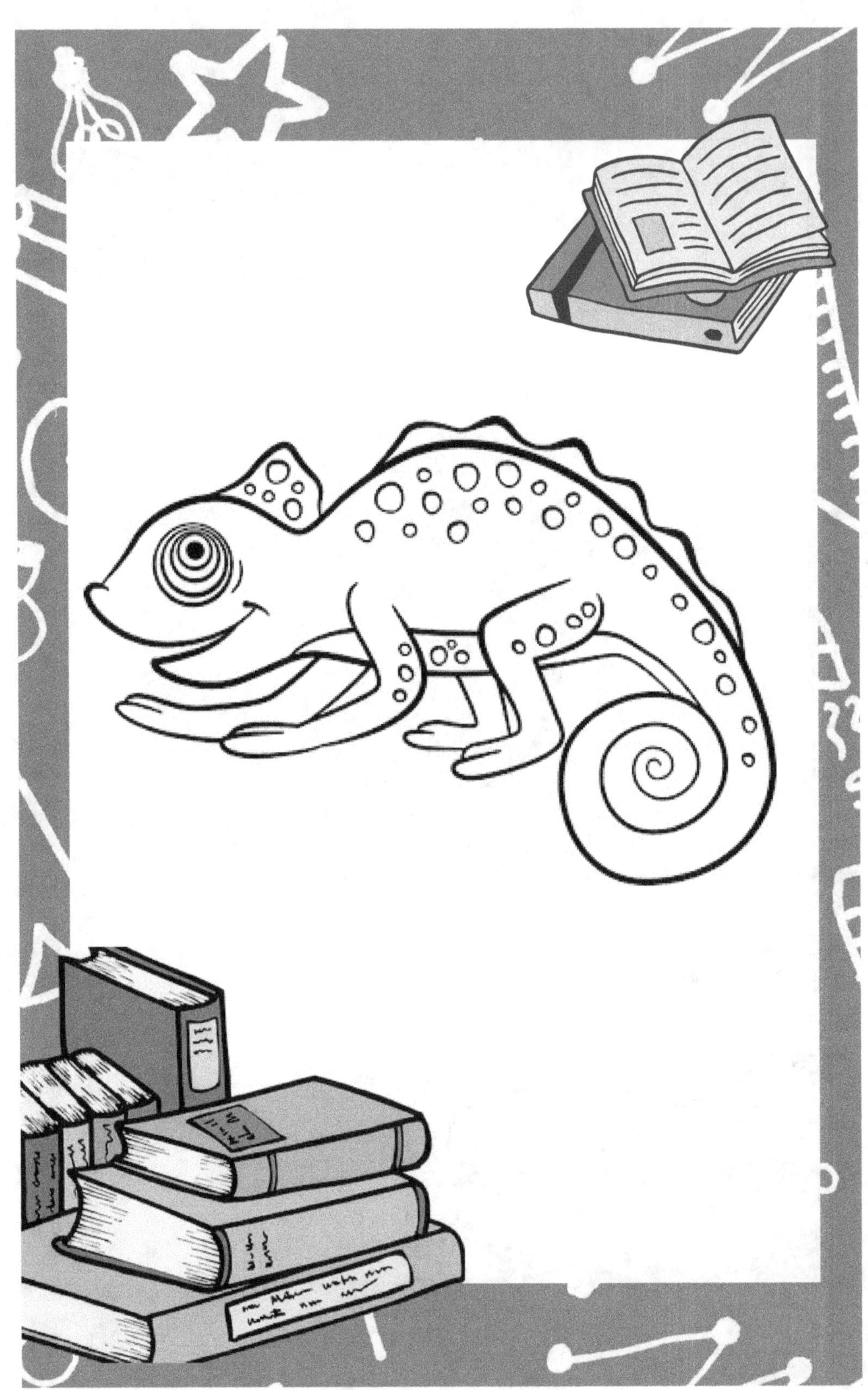

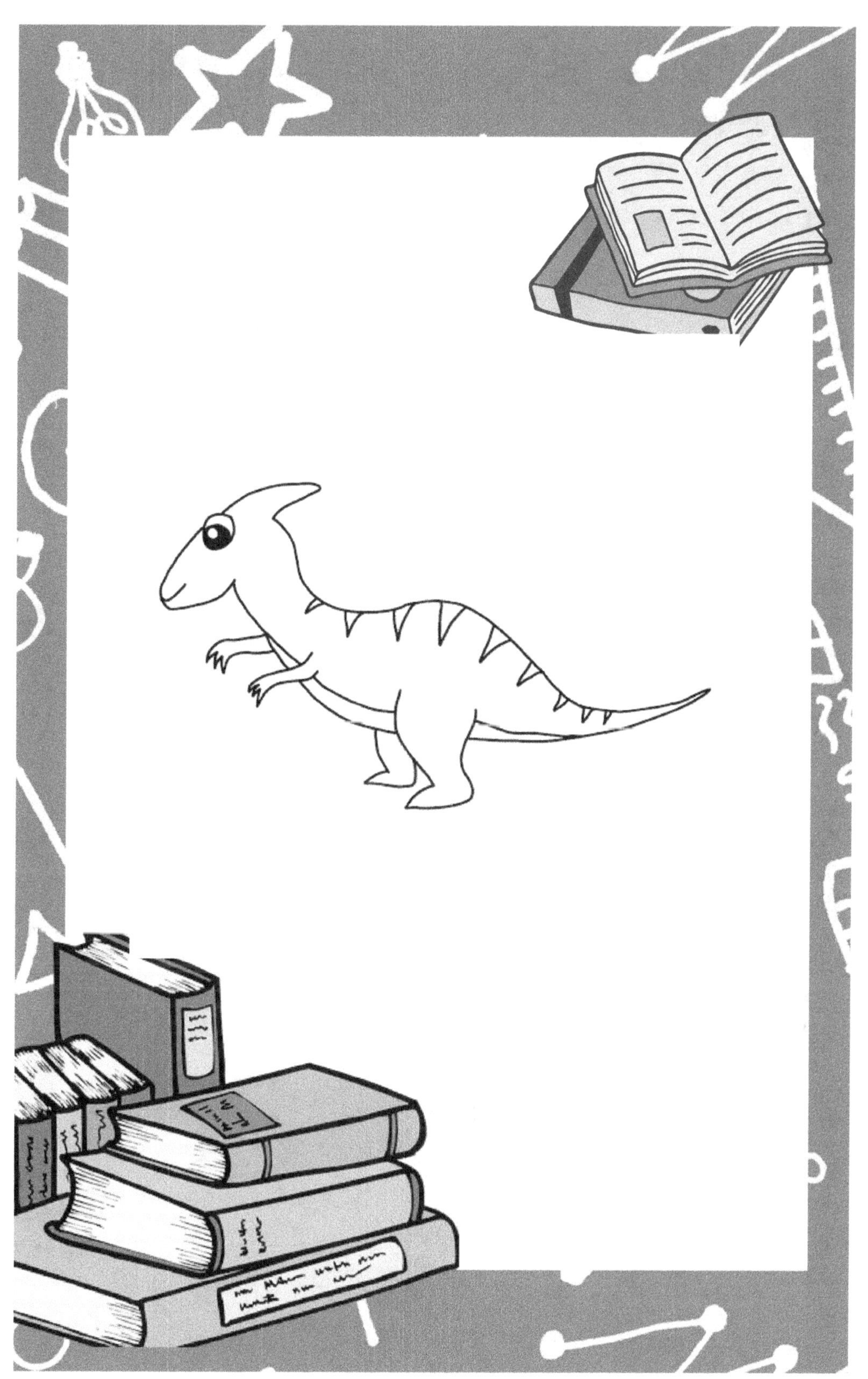

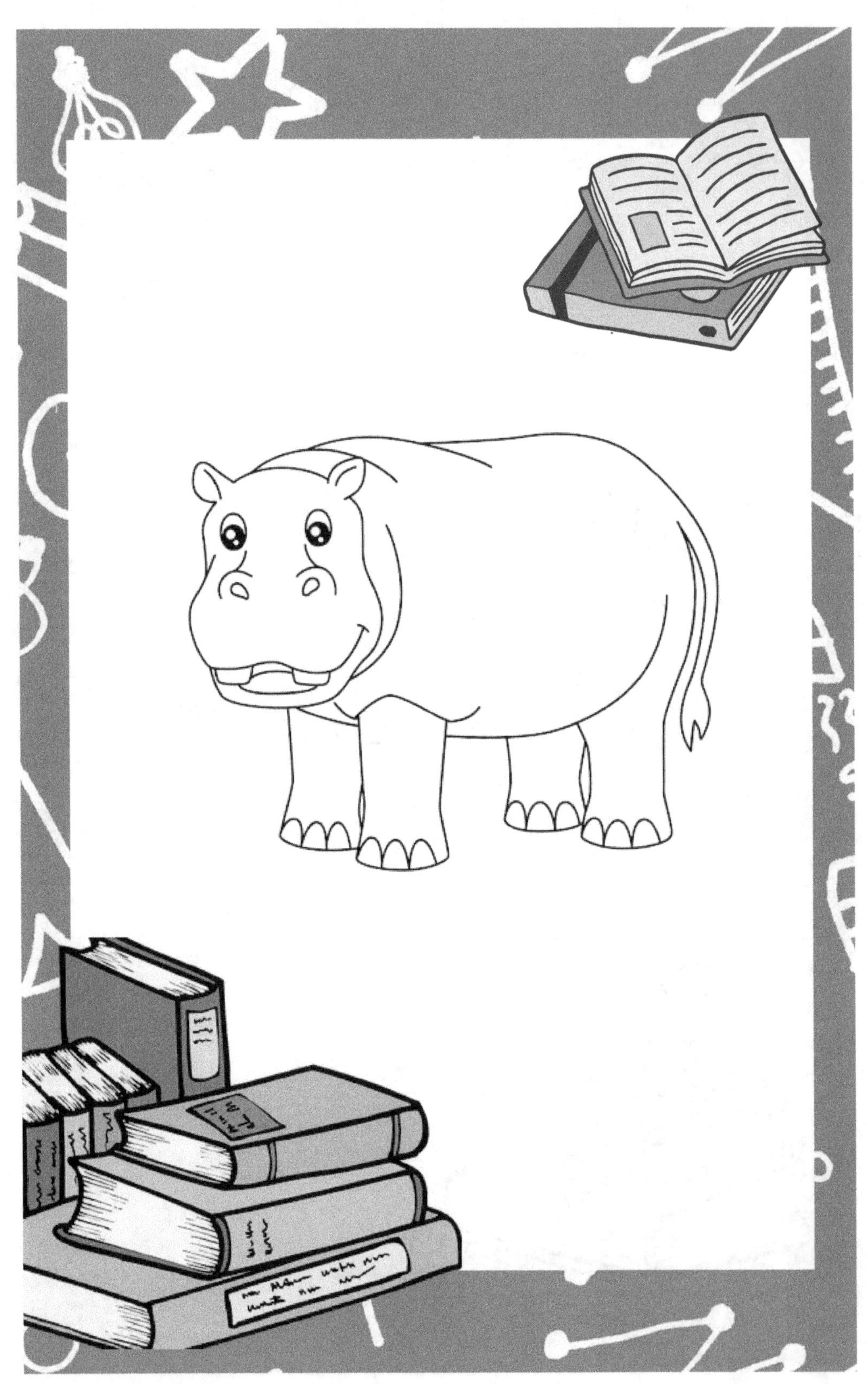

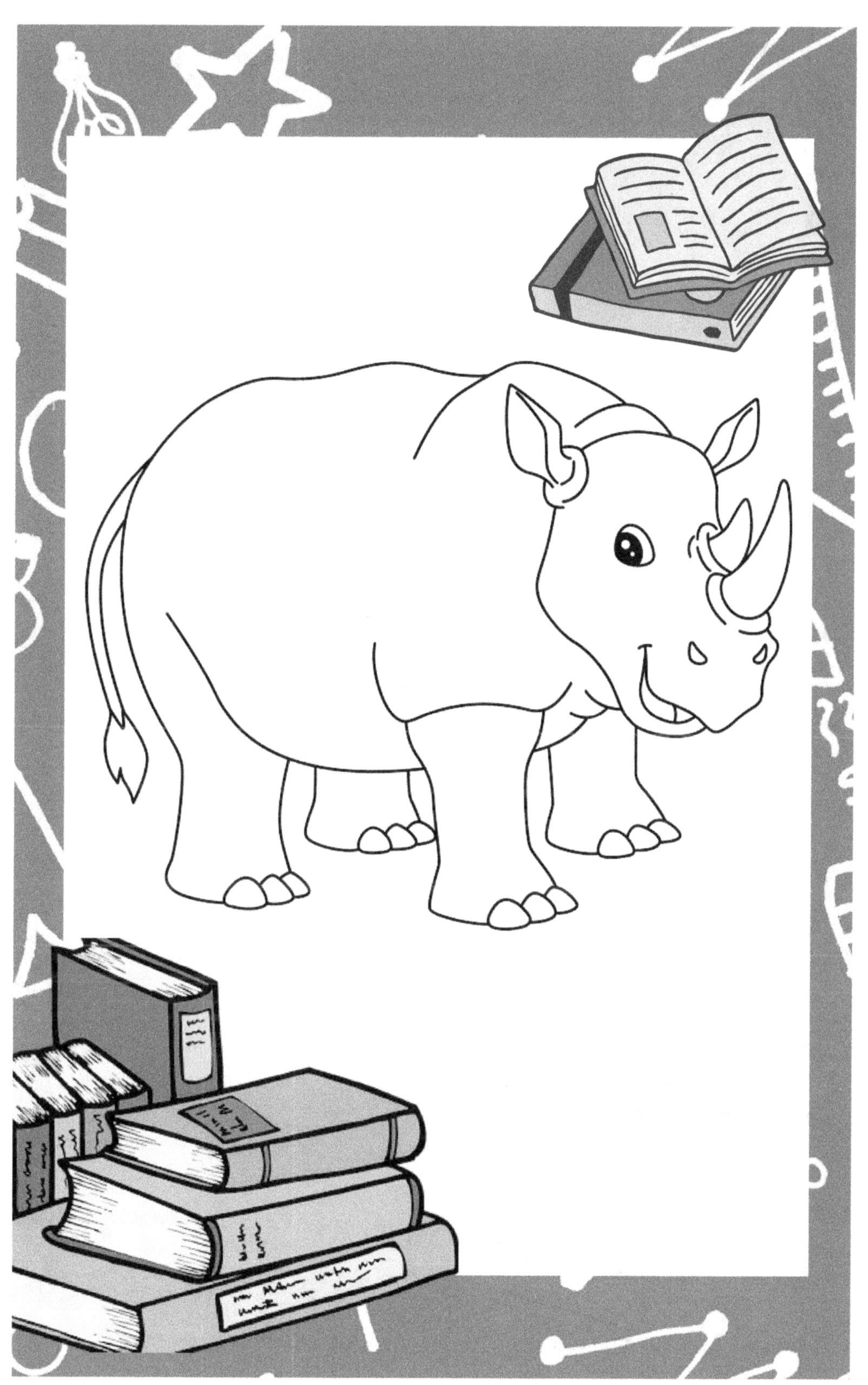

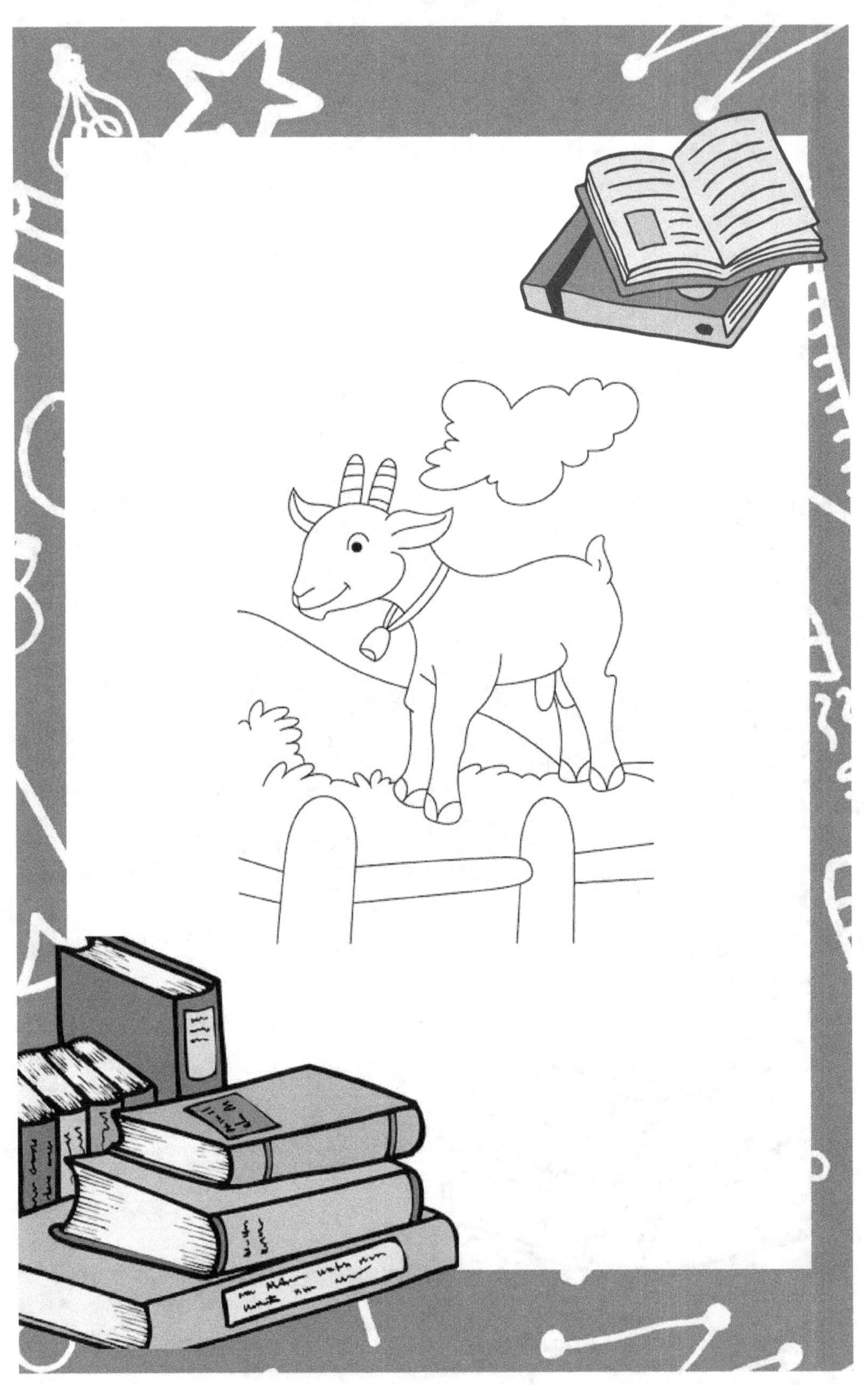

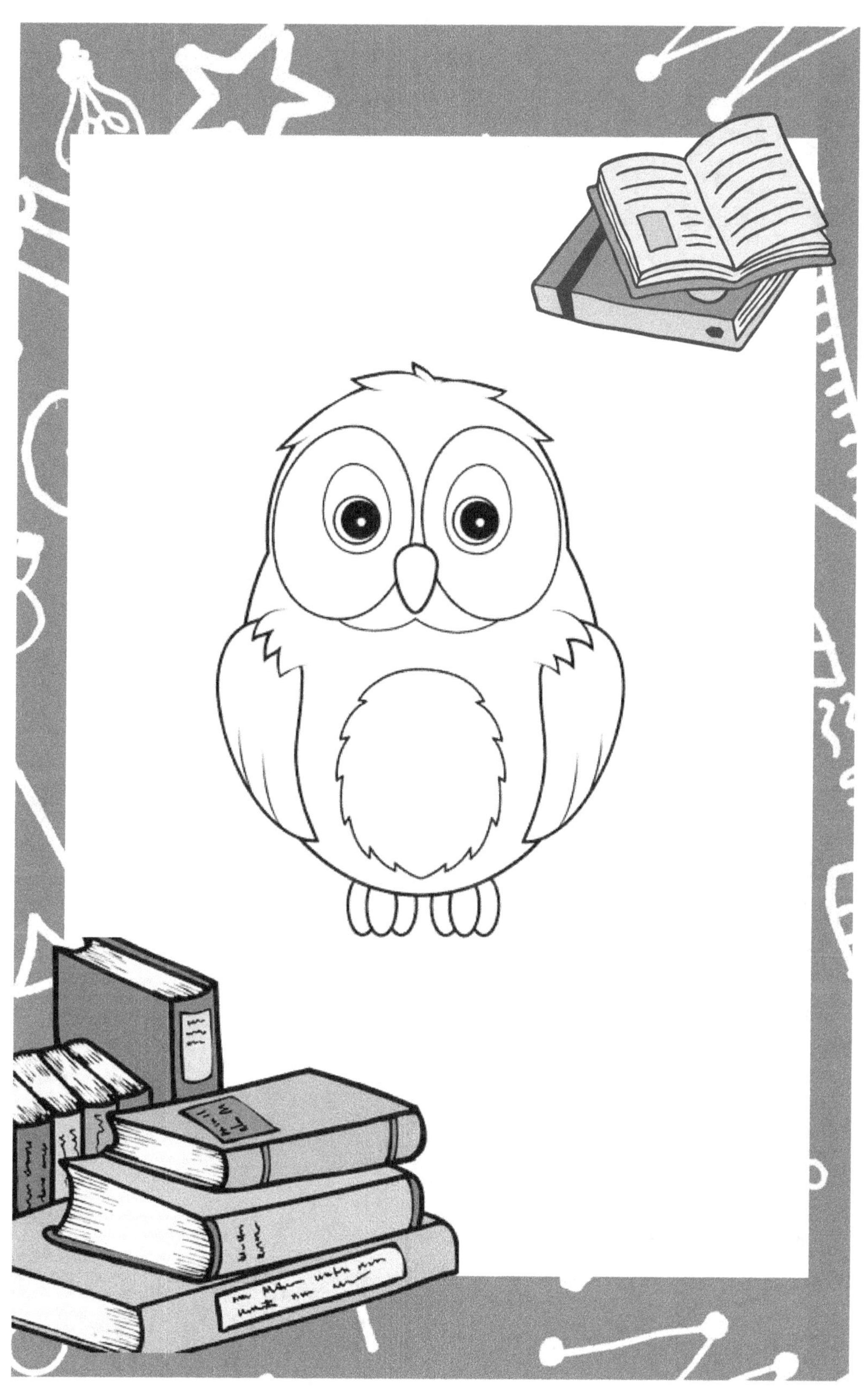

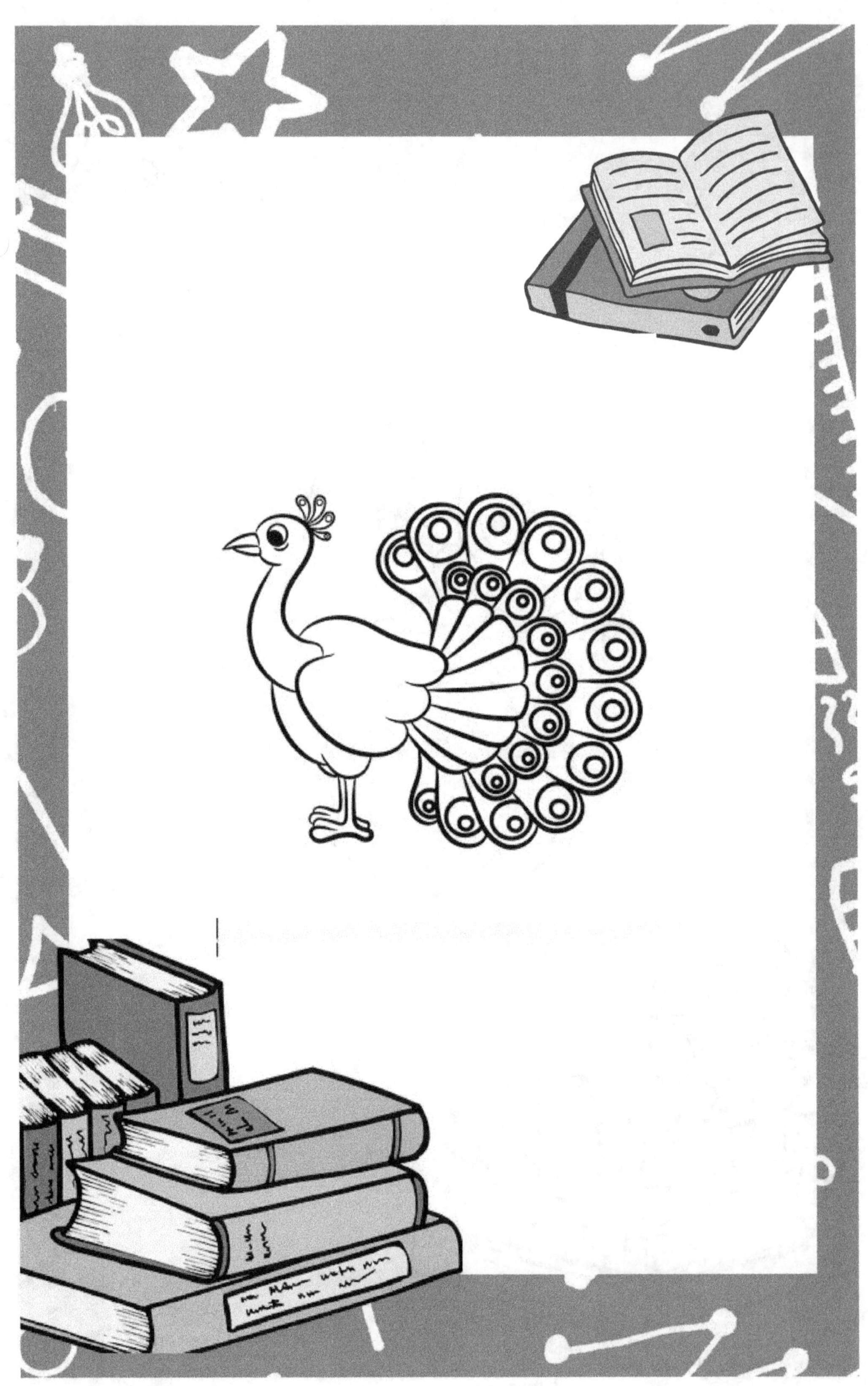

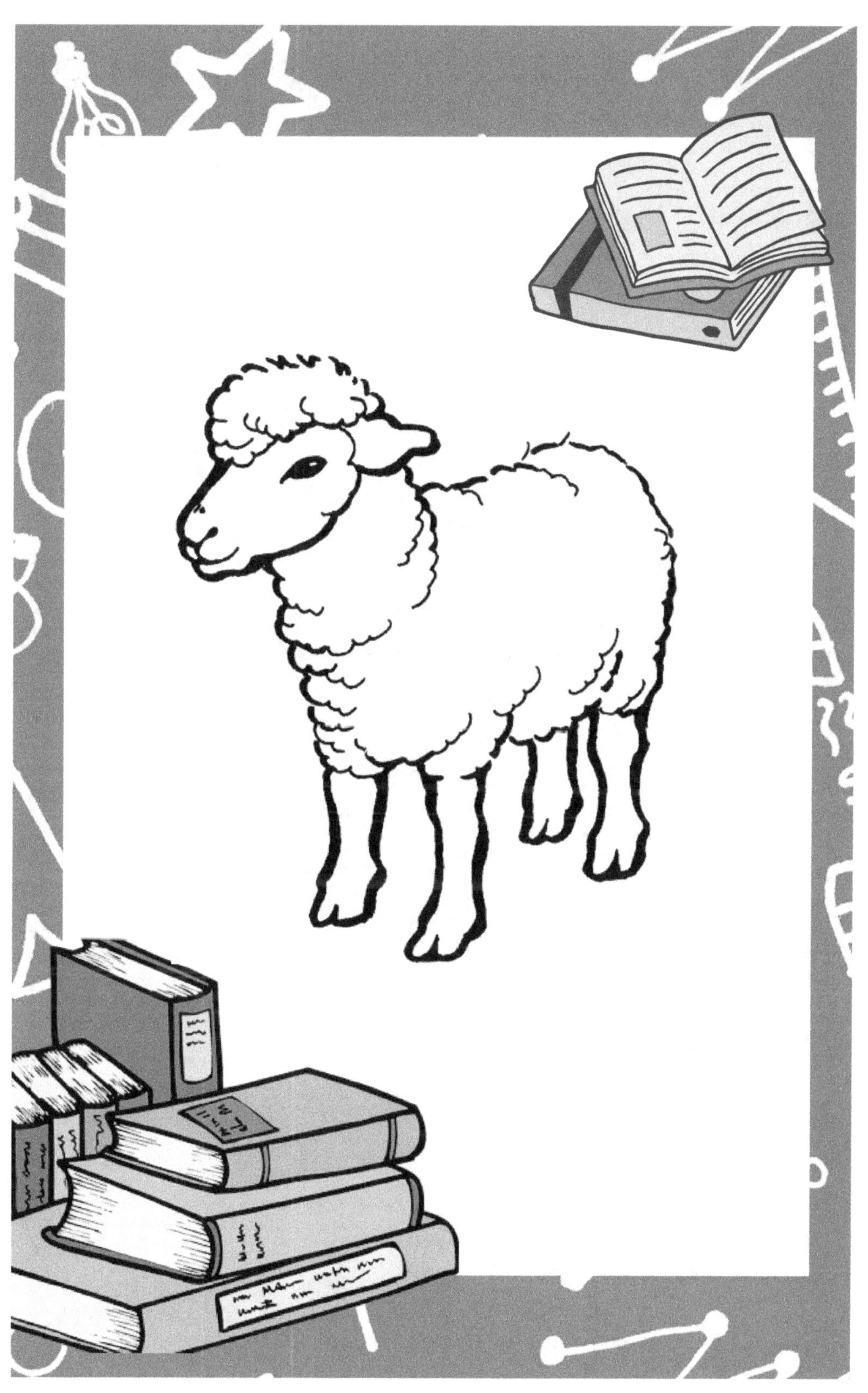

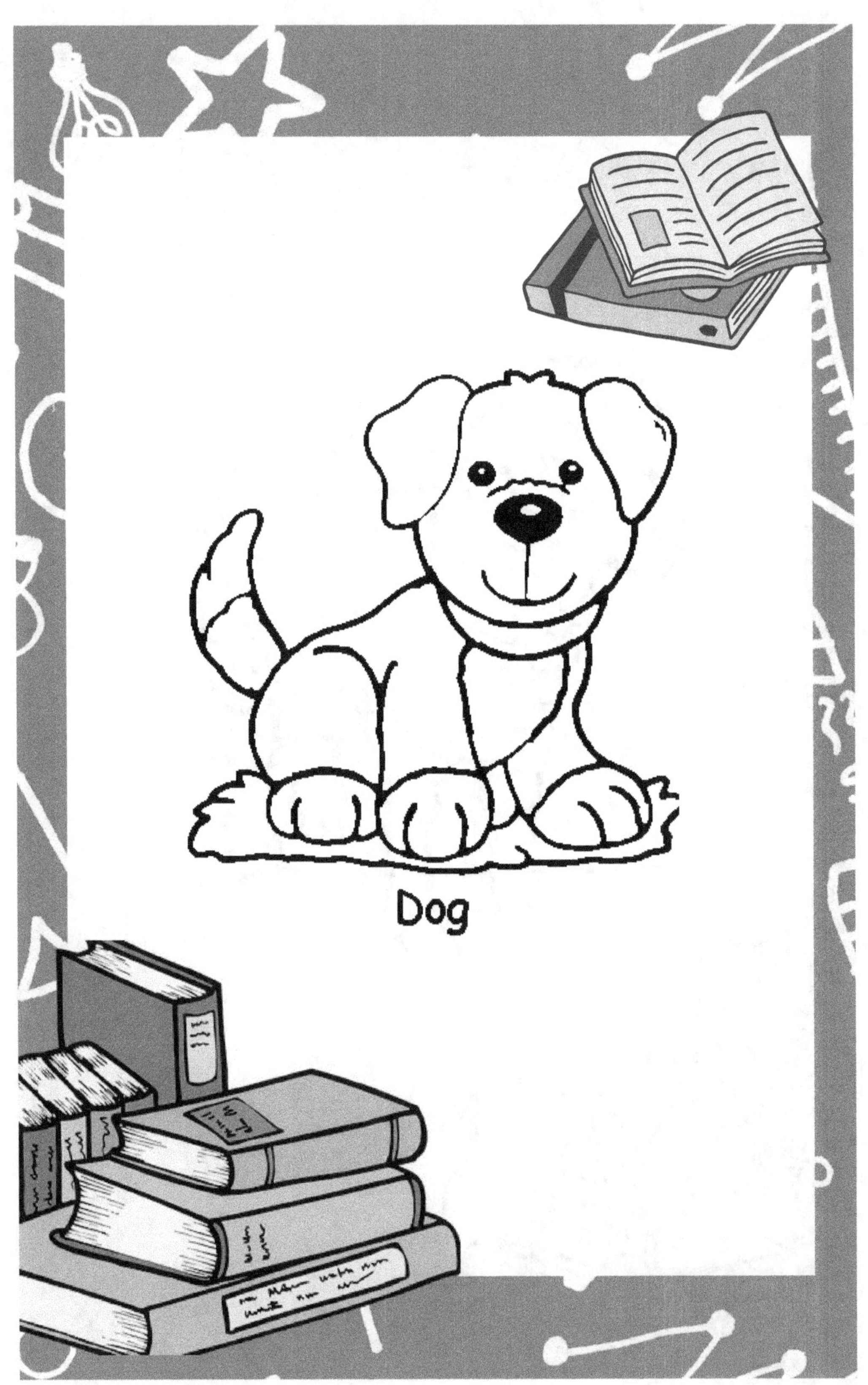

Dog

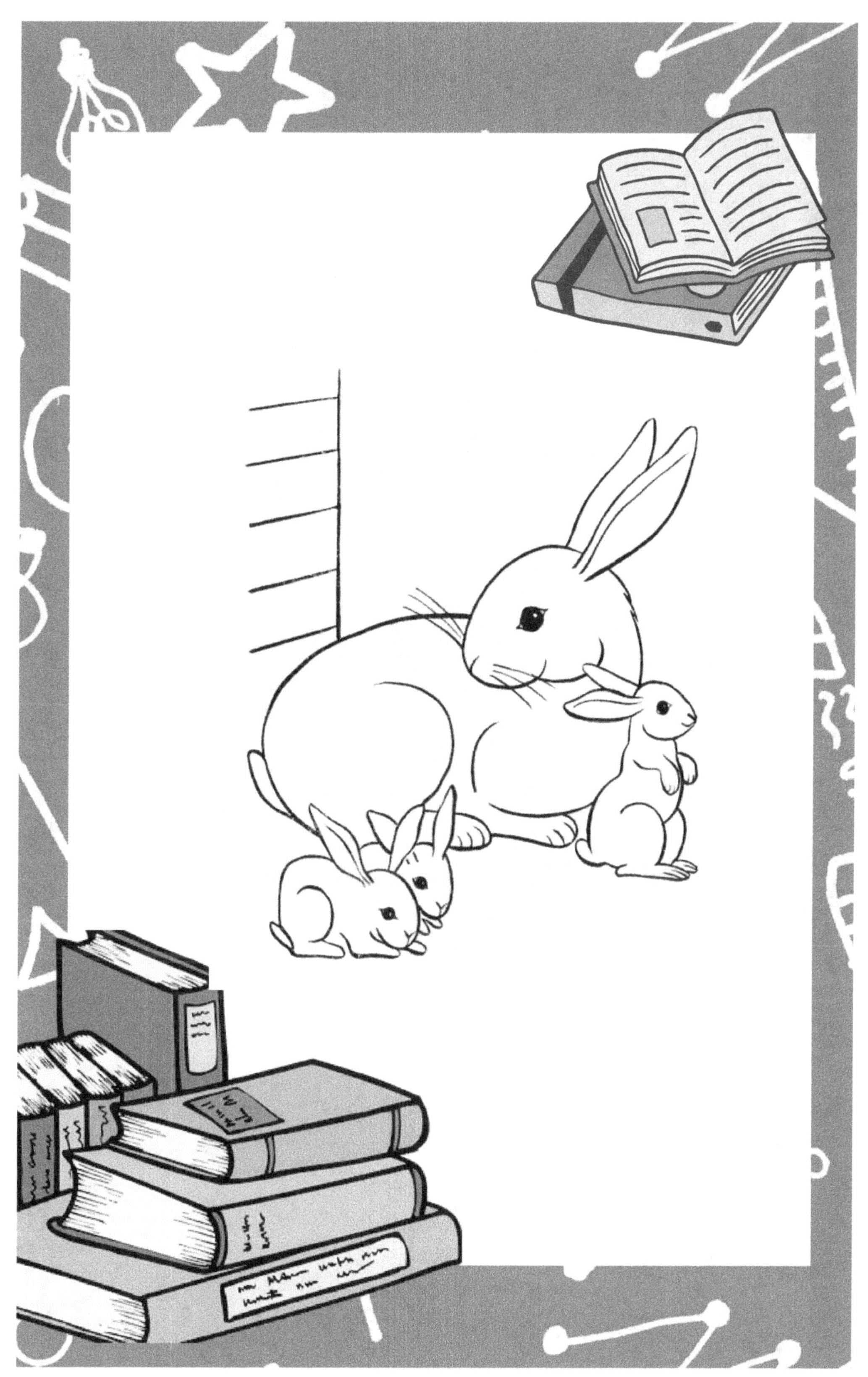

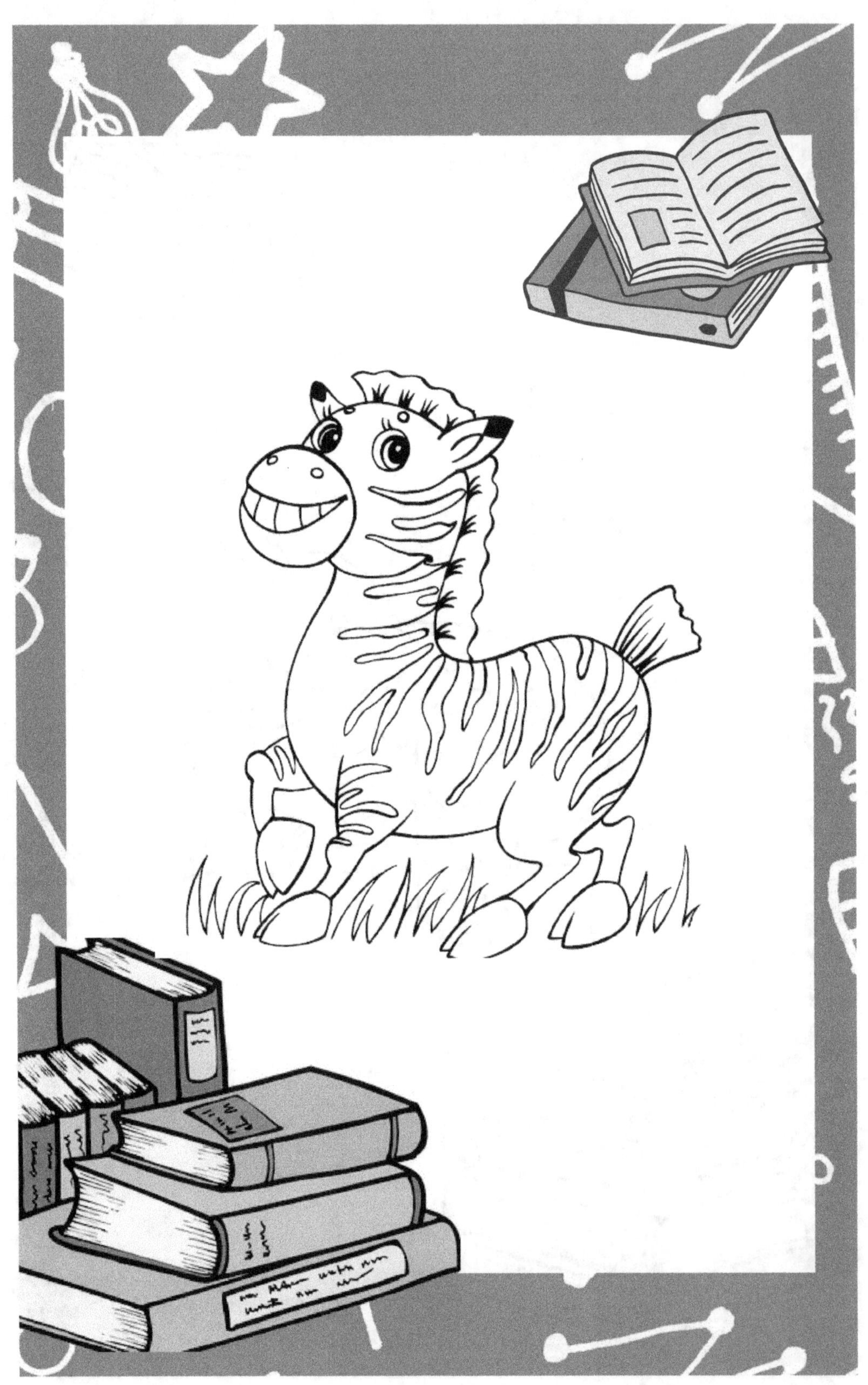

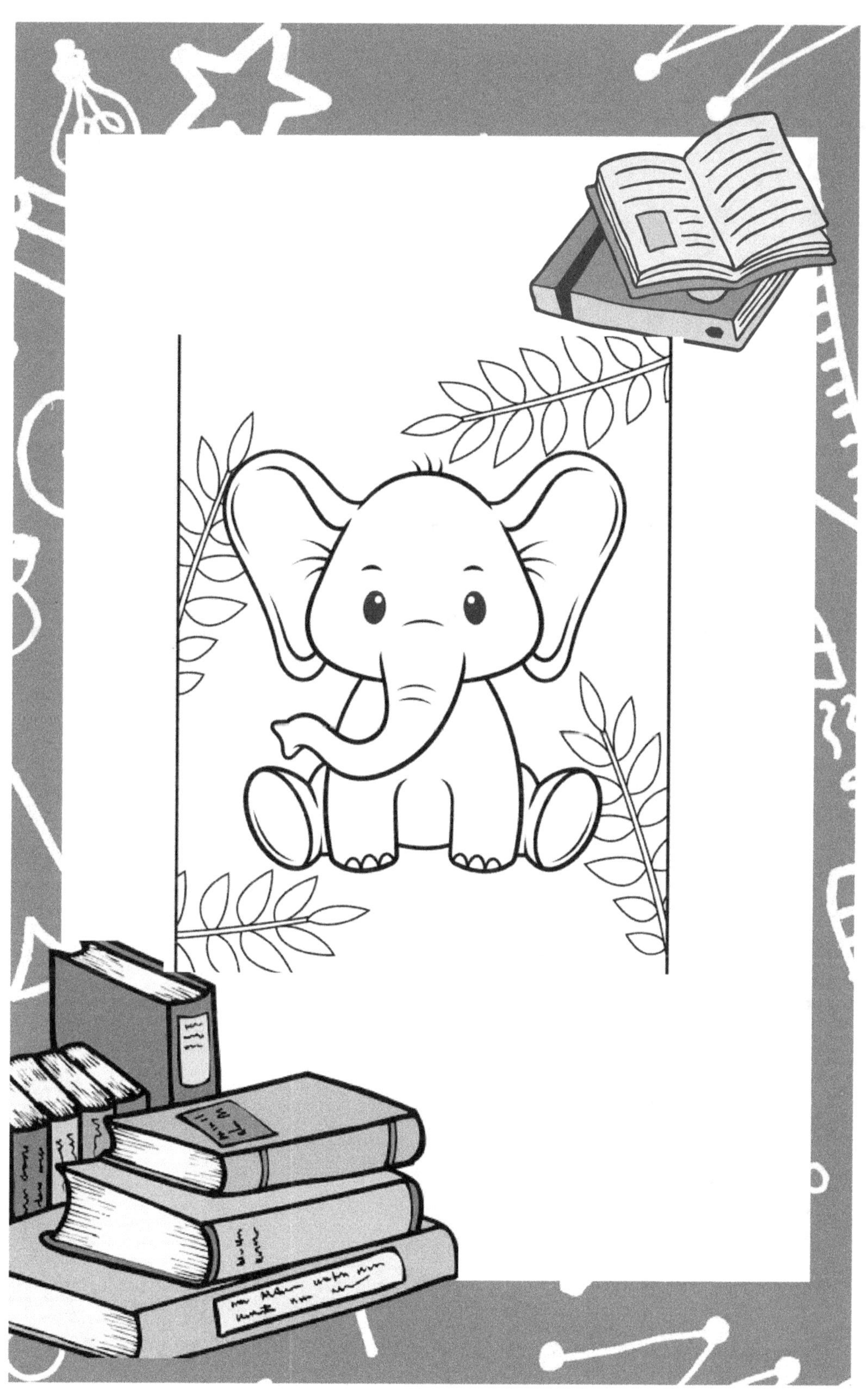

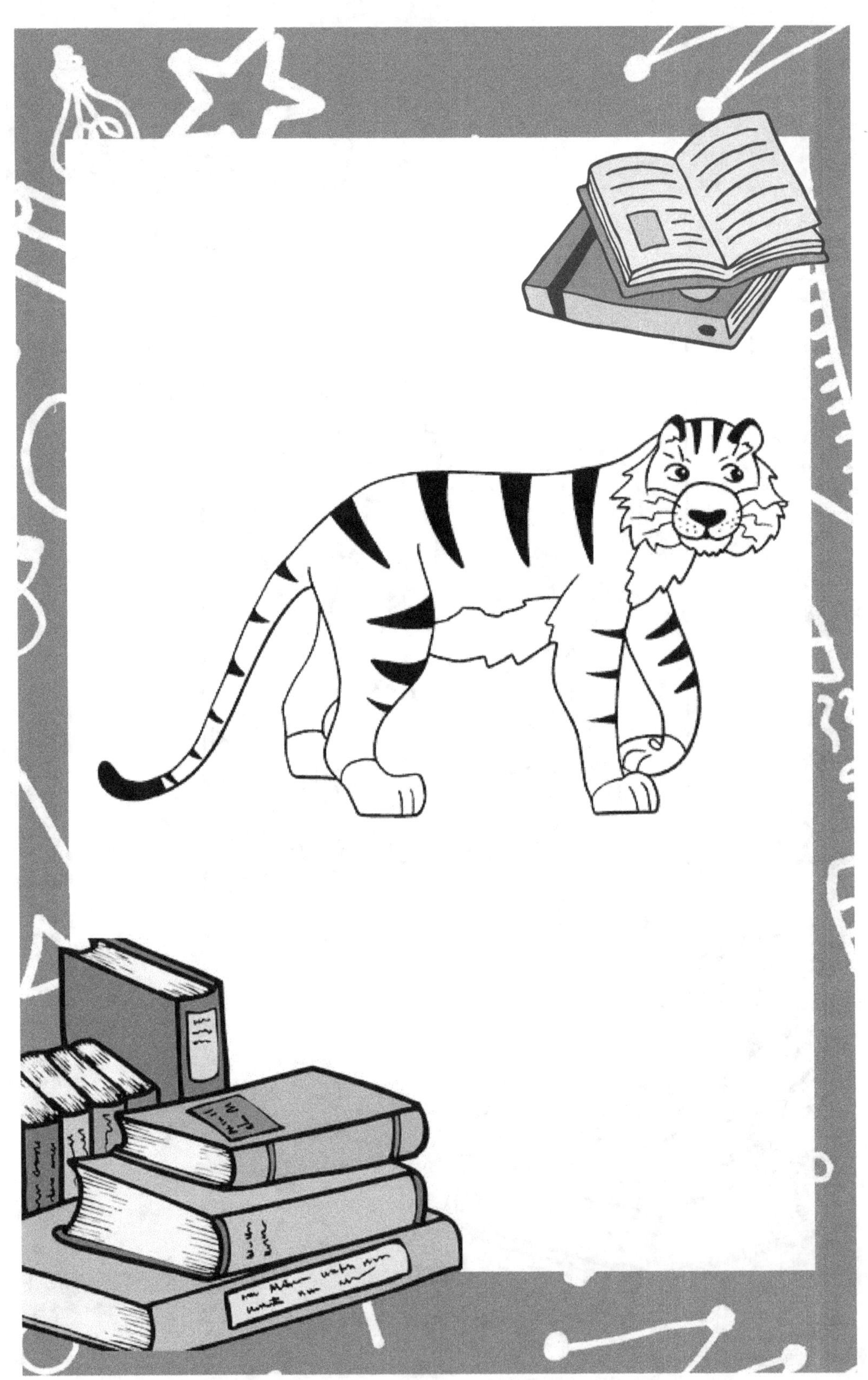

Cats

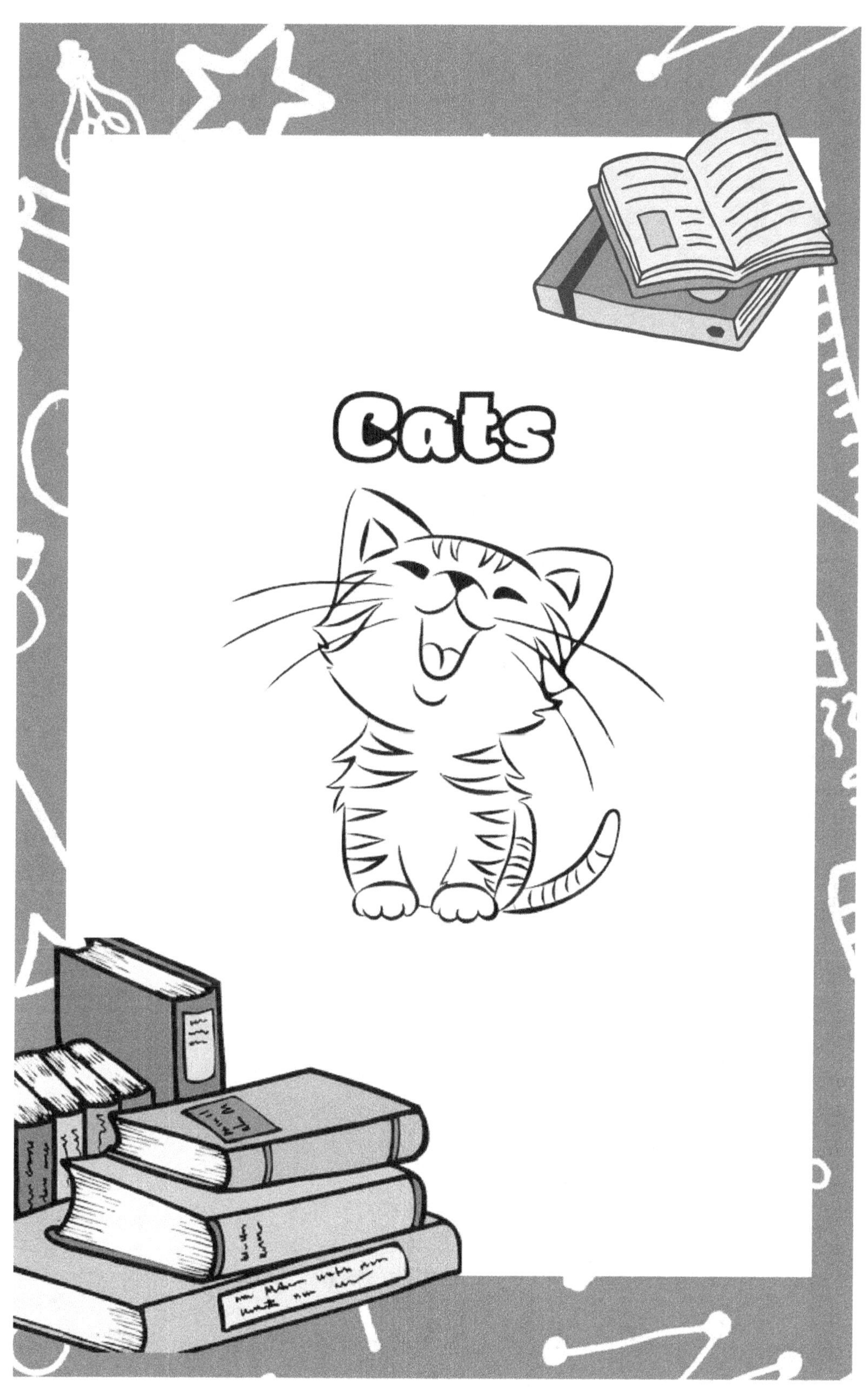

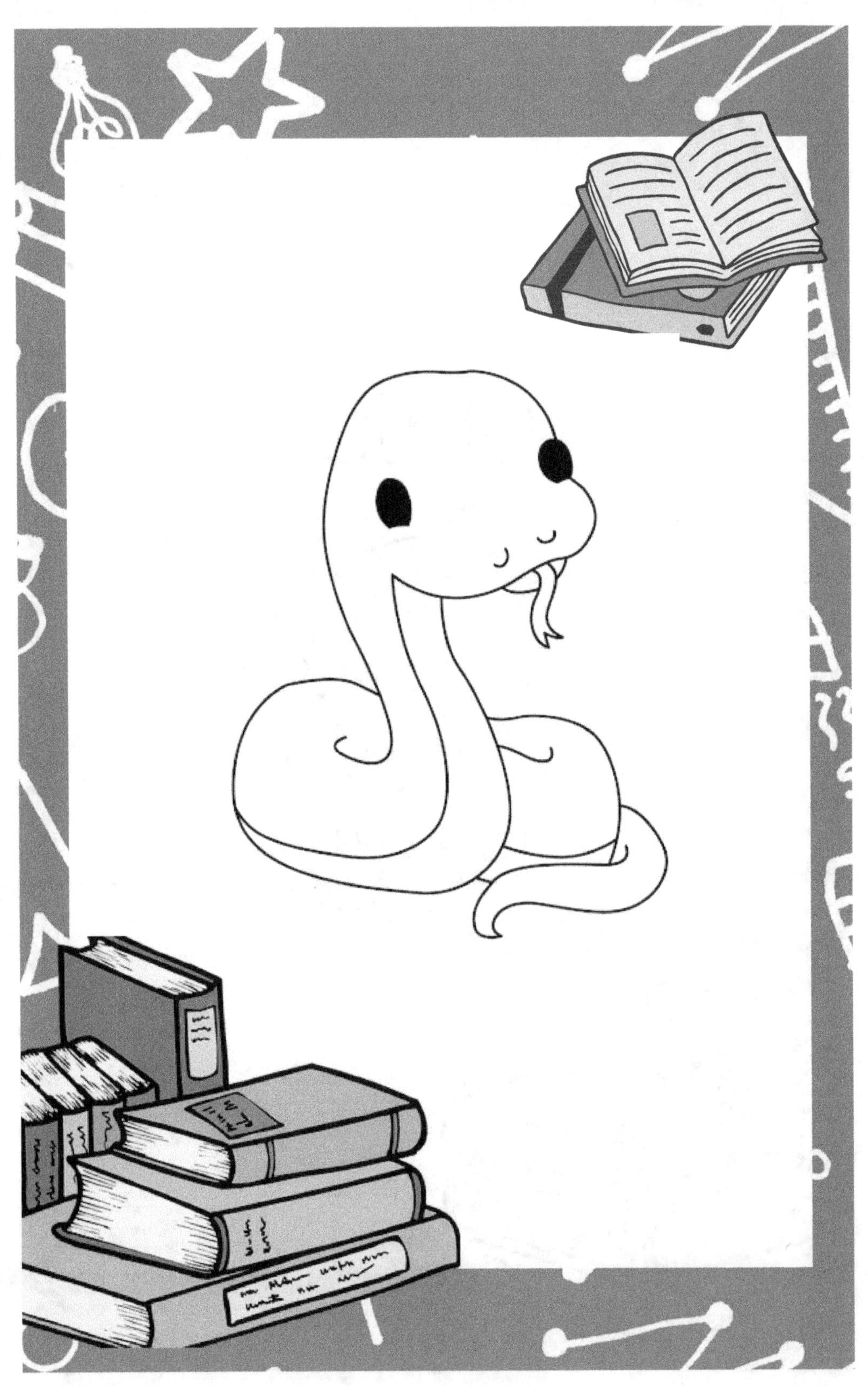

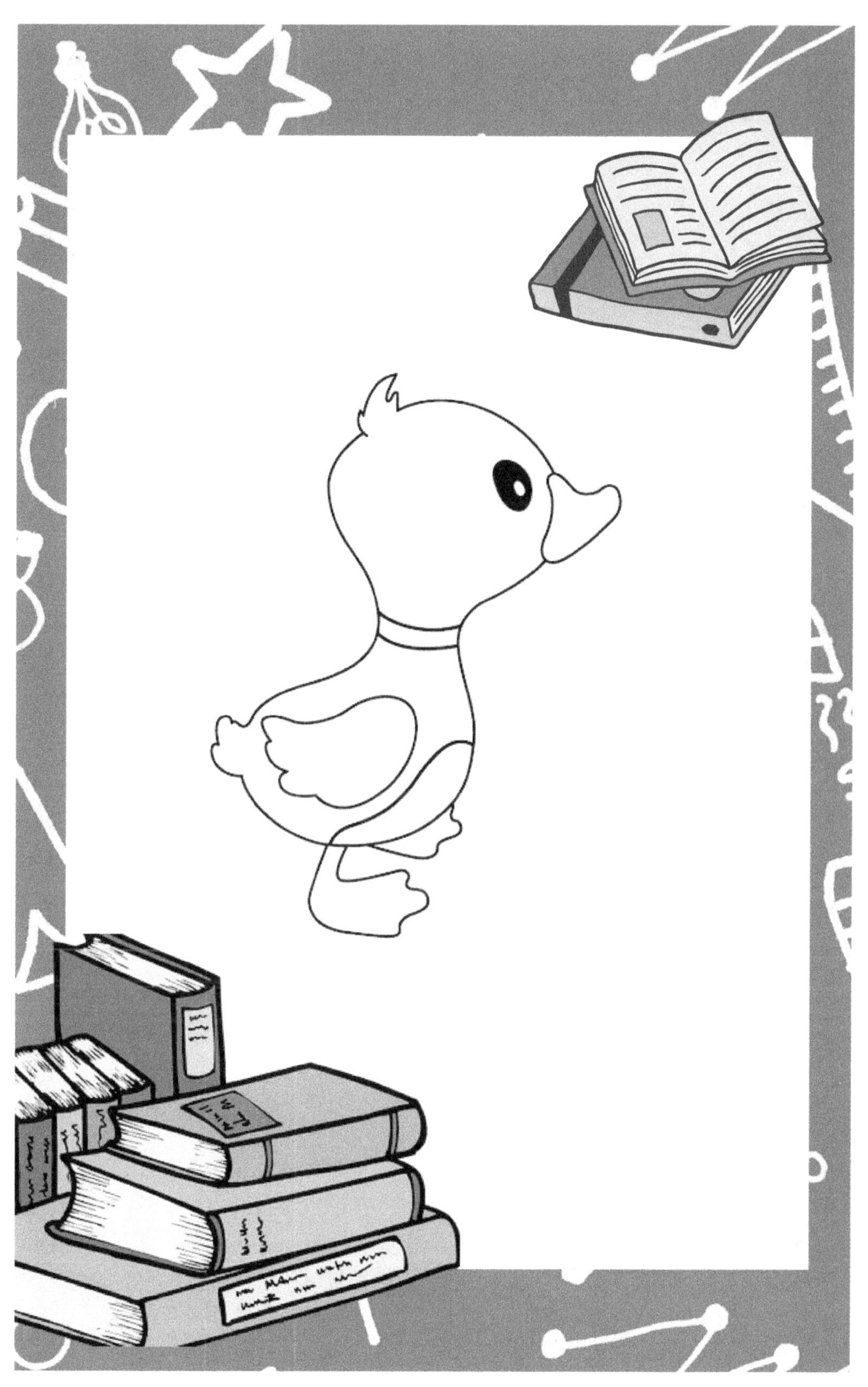

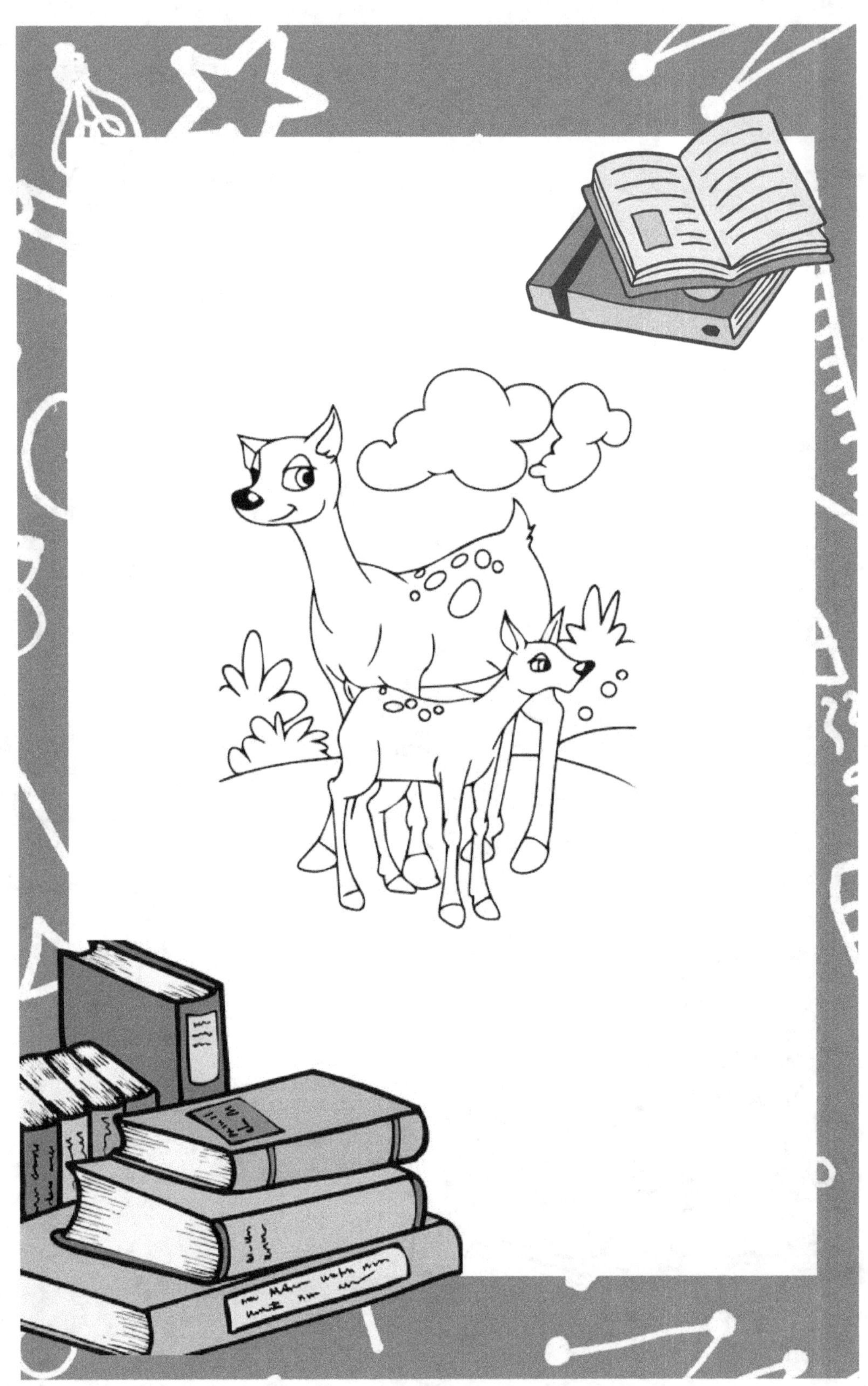

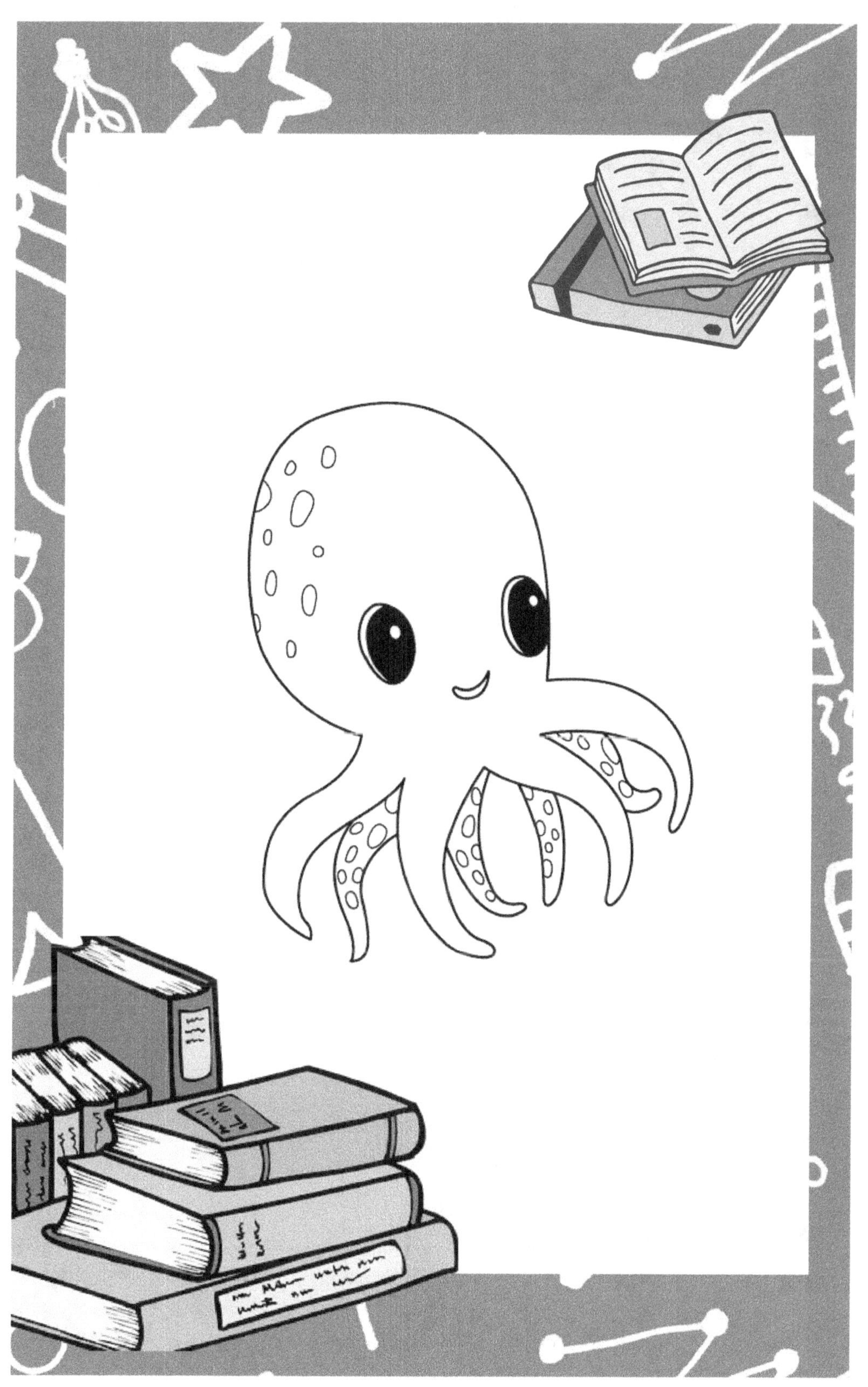

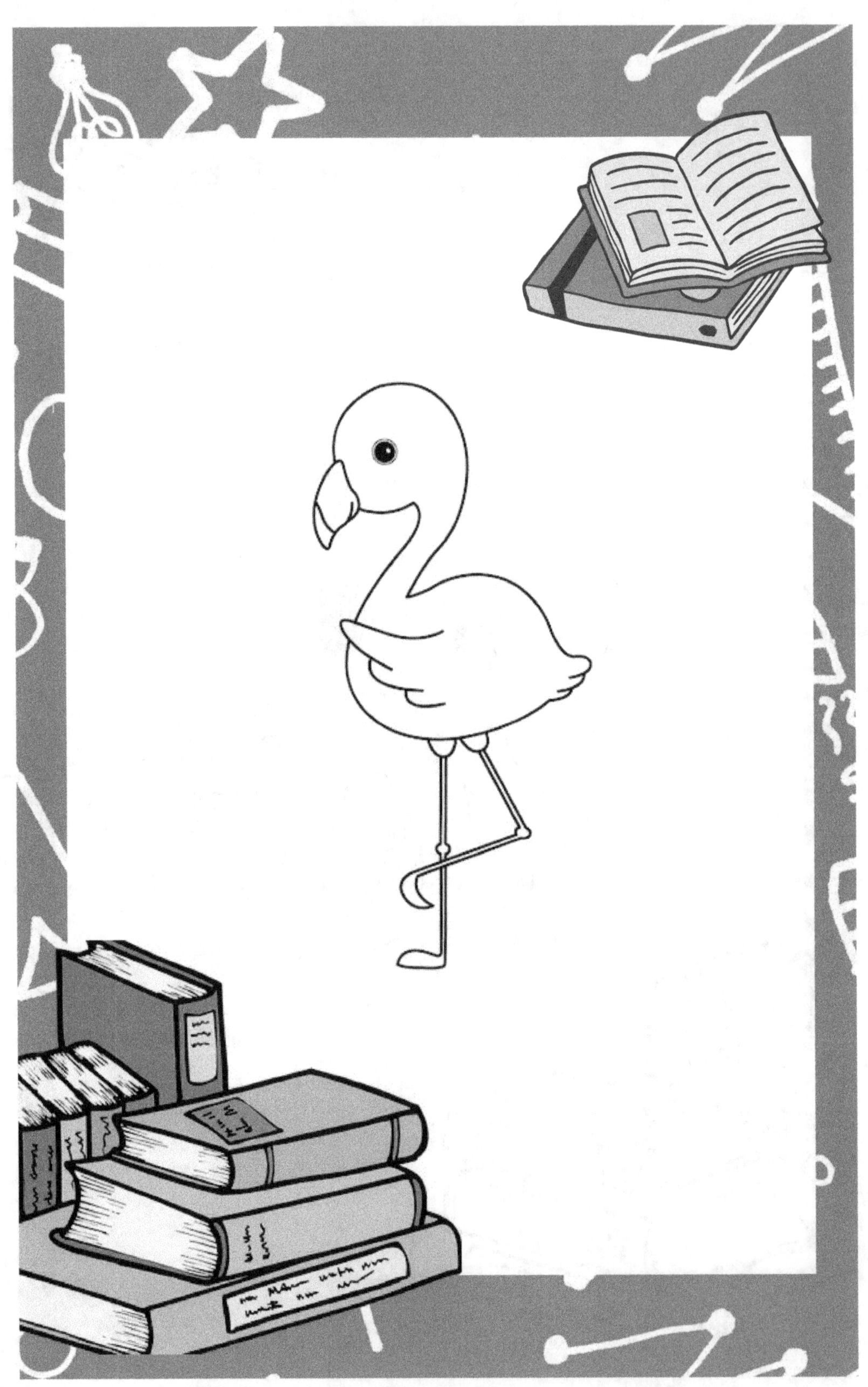

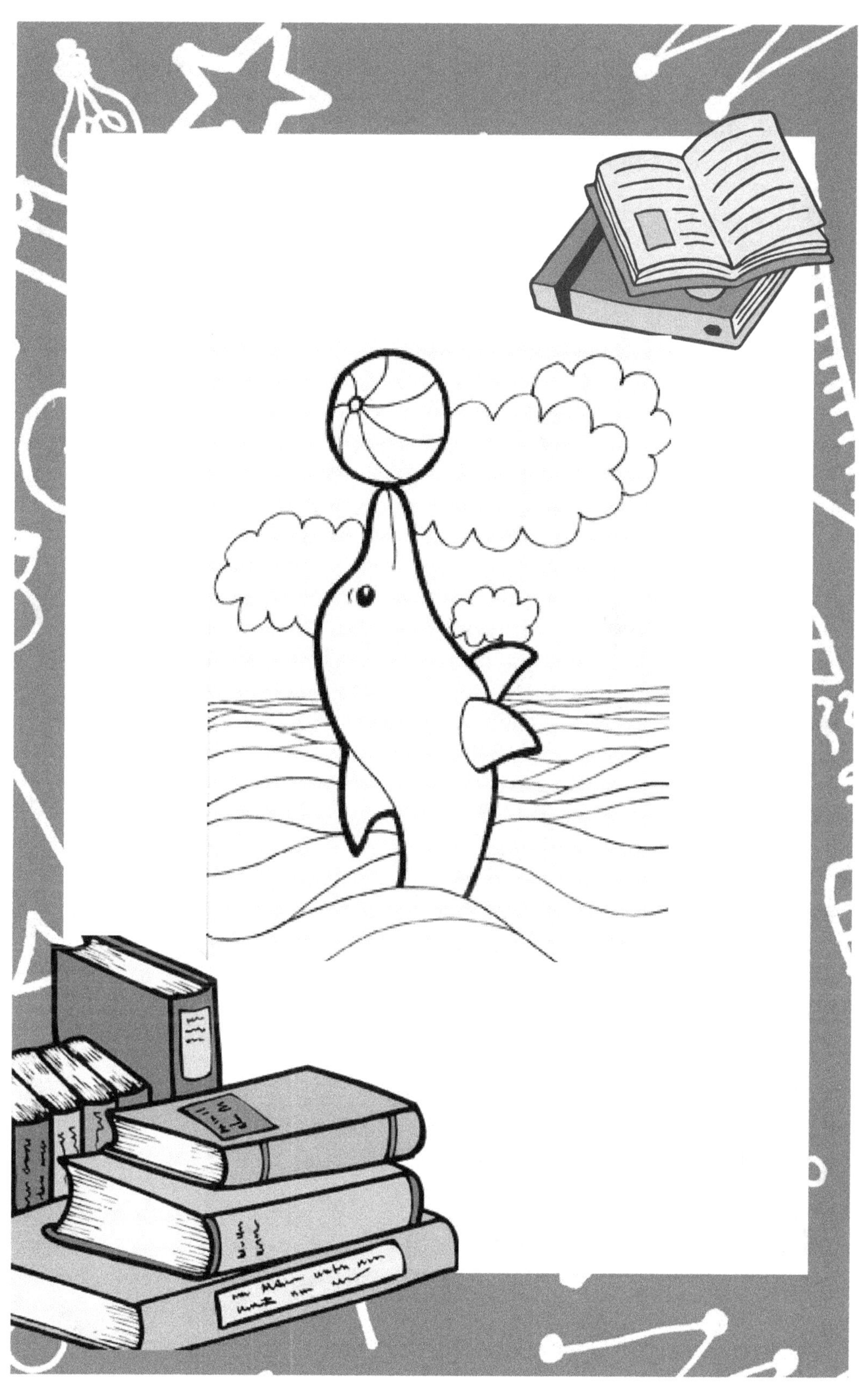

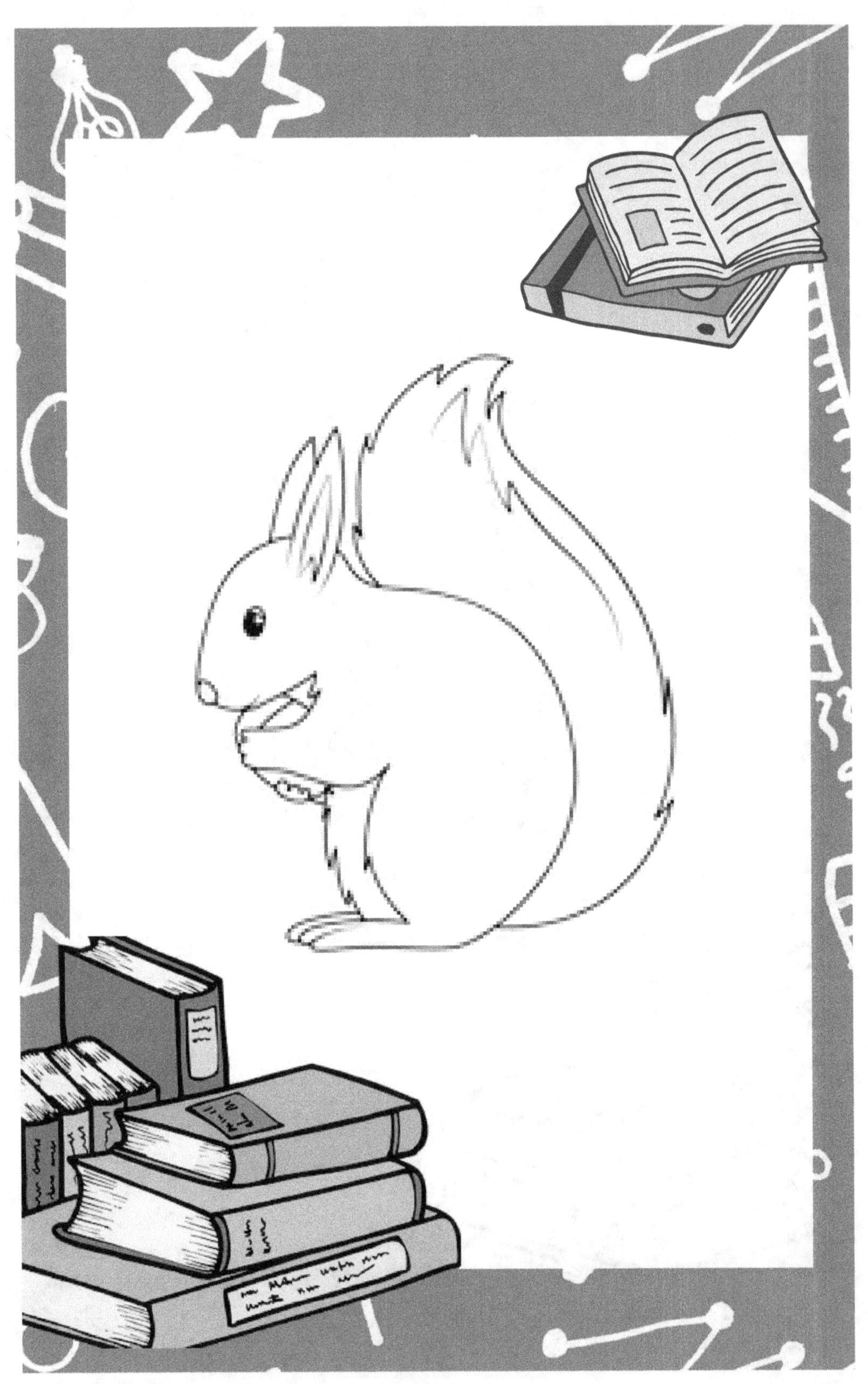

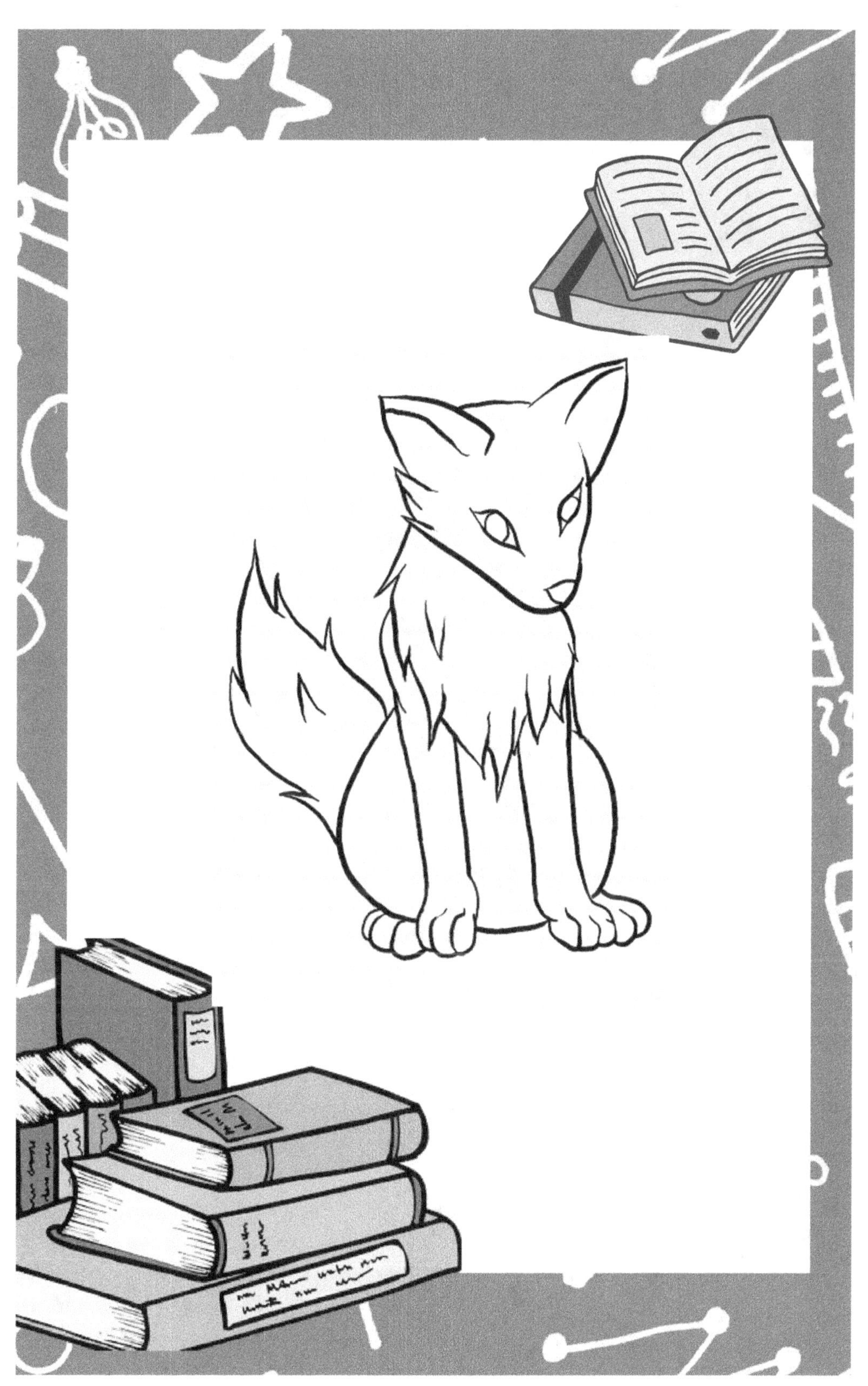

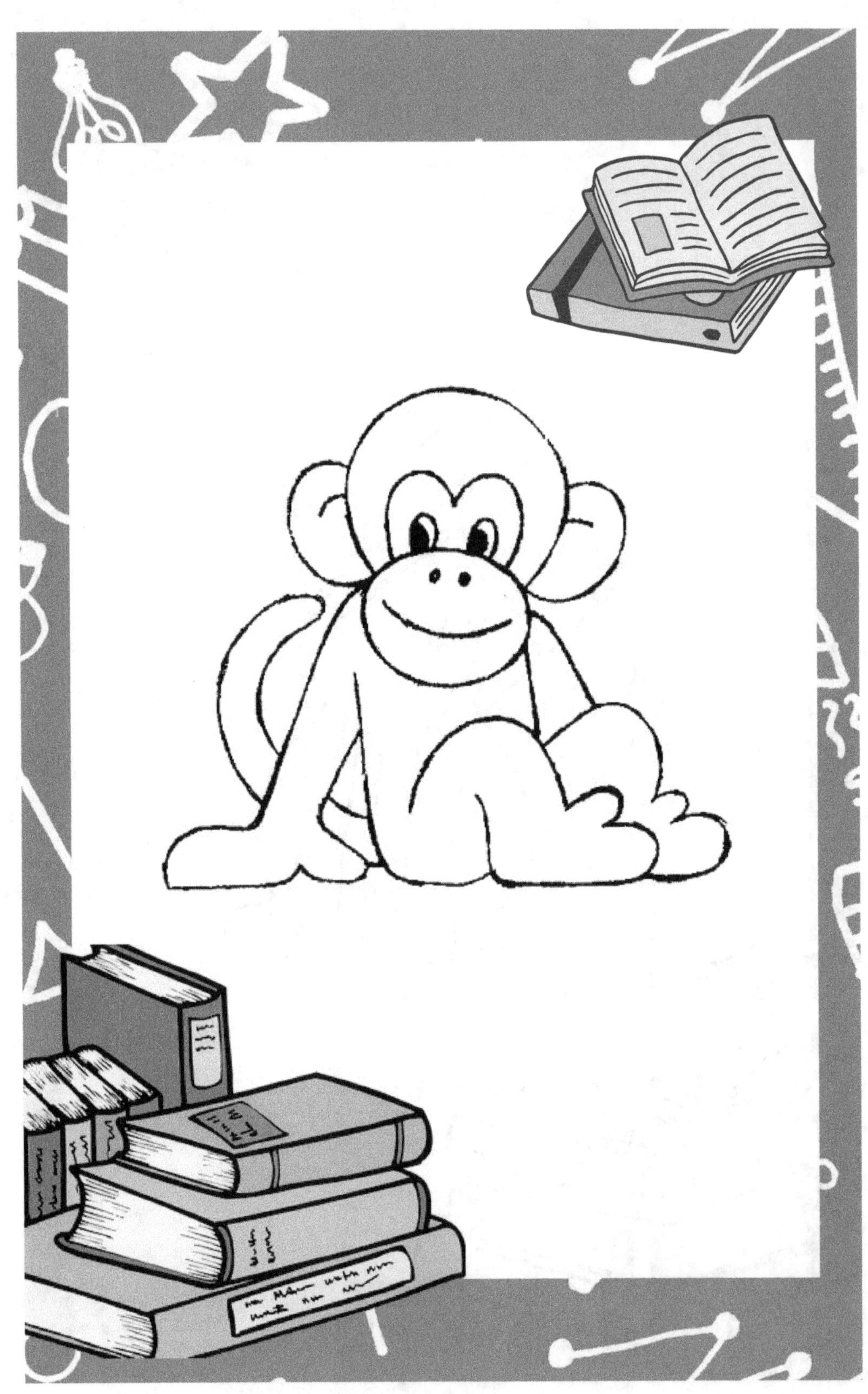

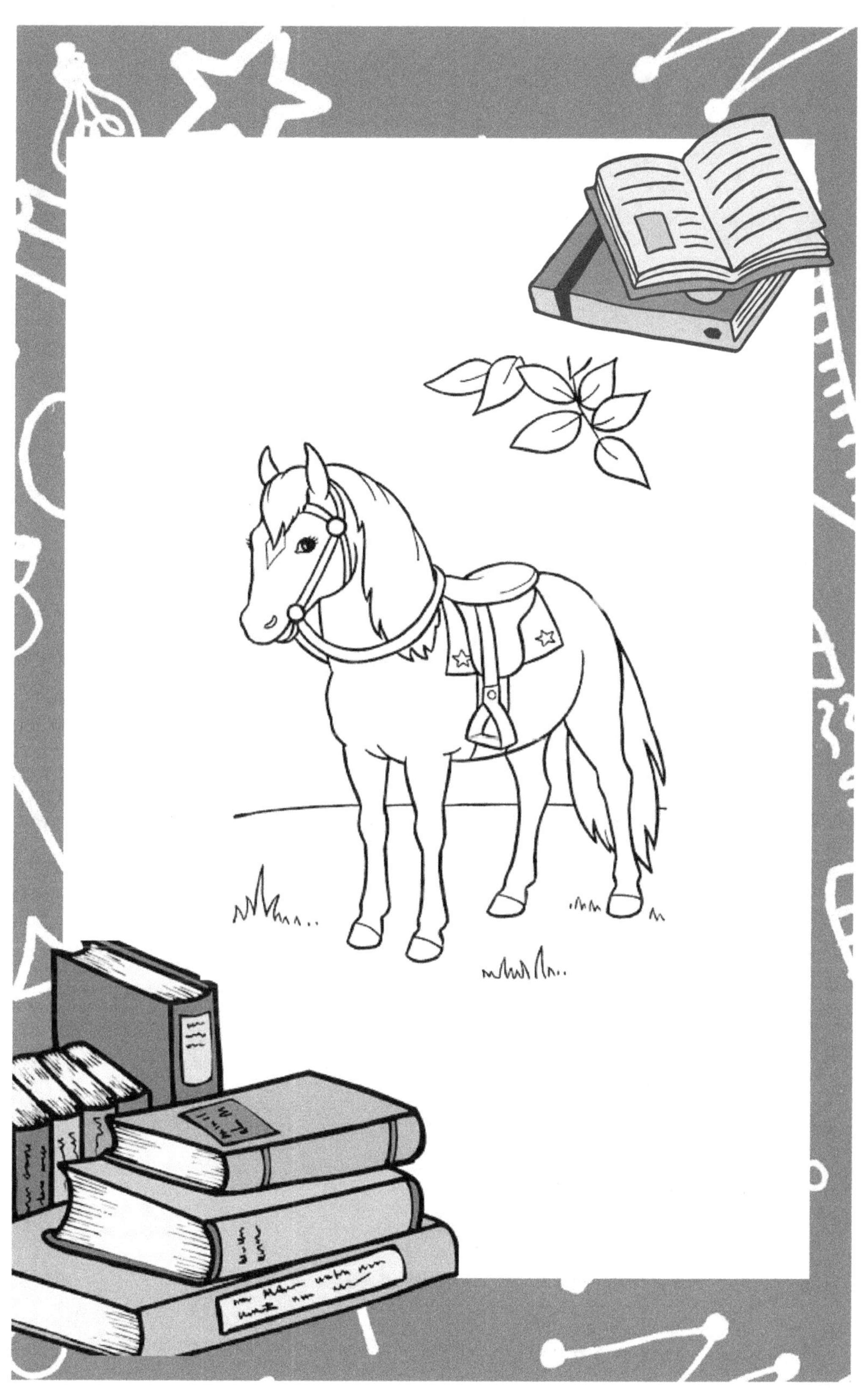

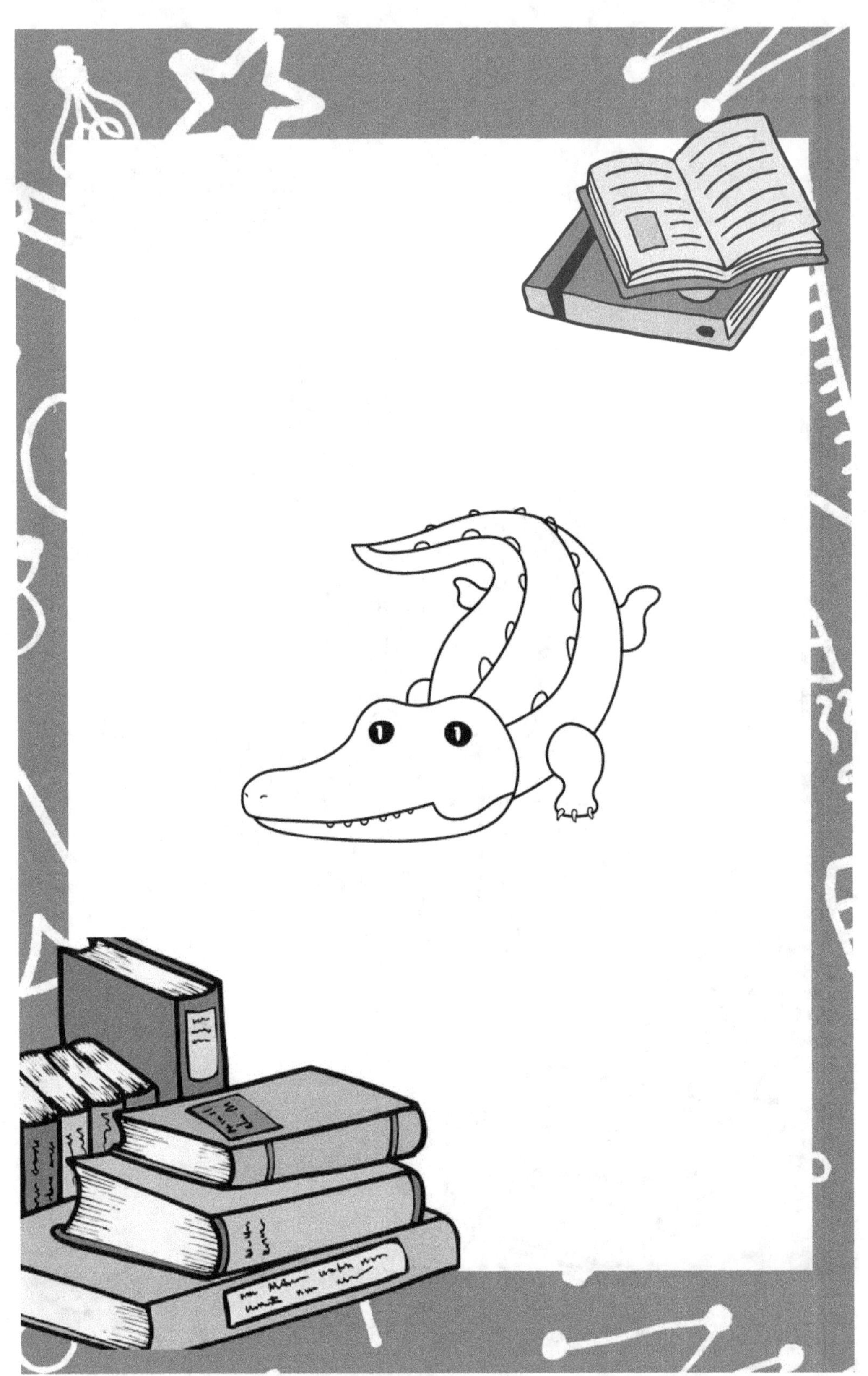

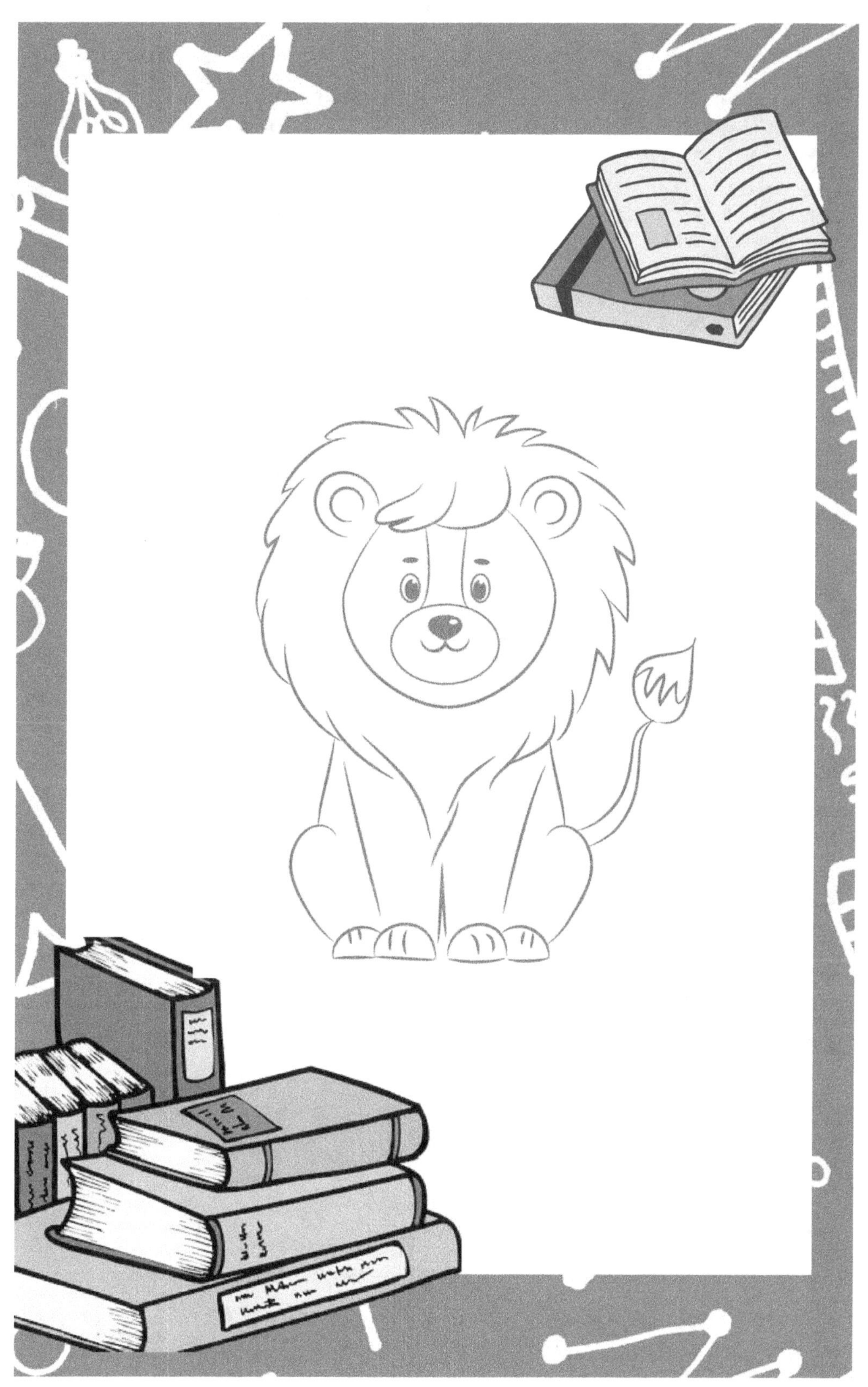

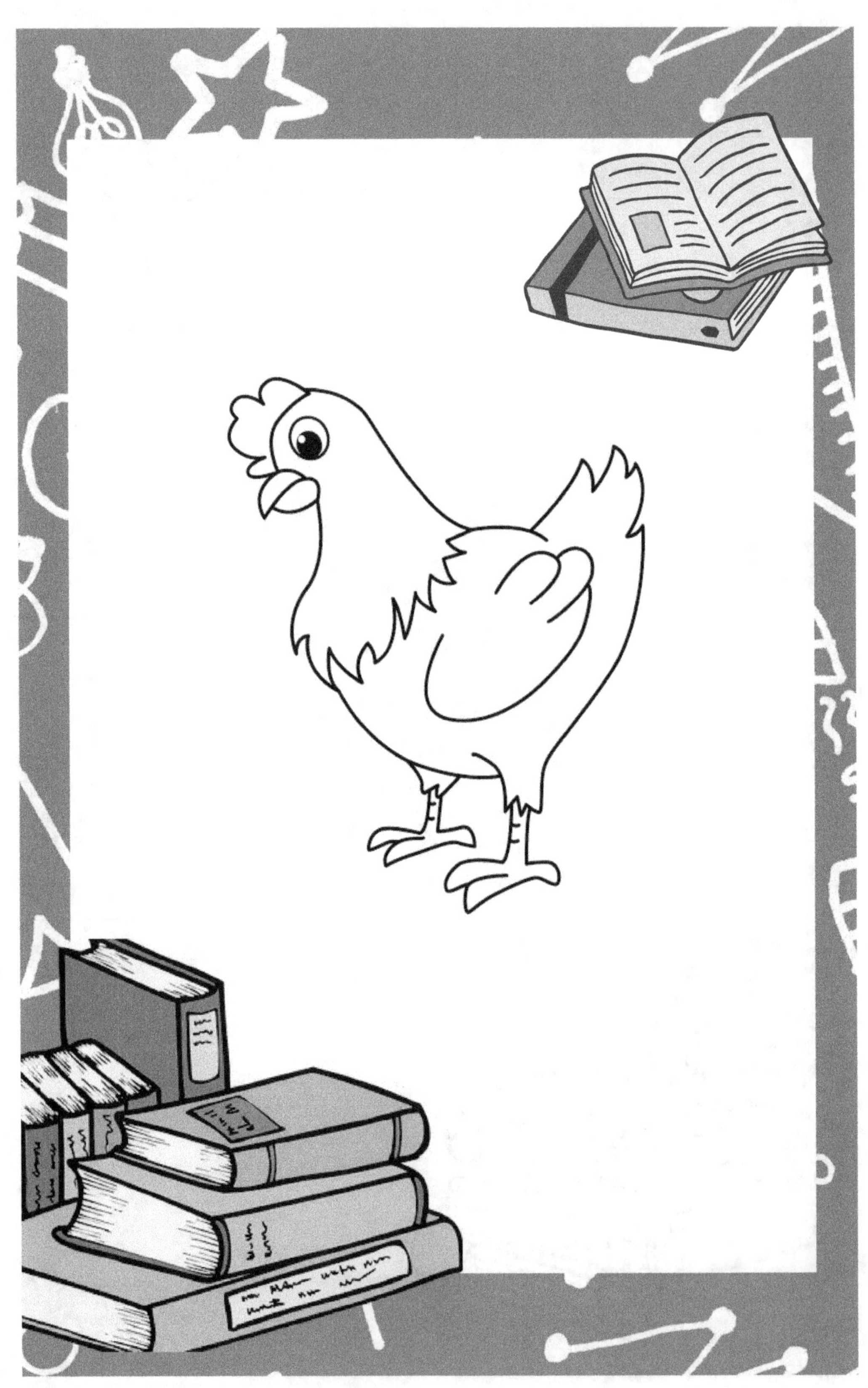

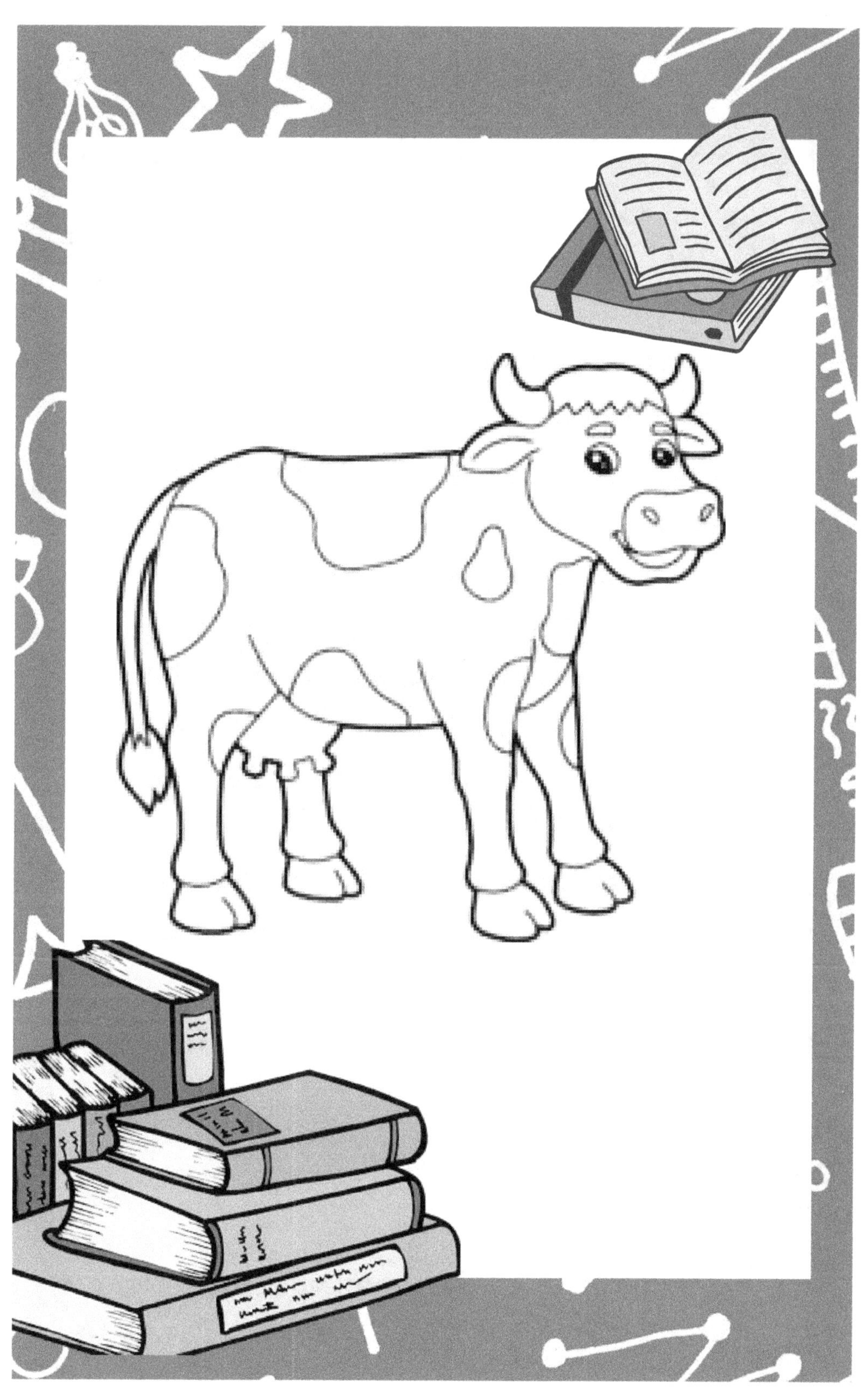

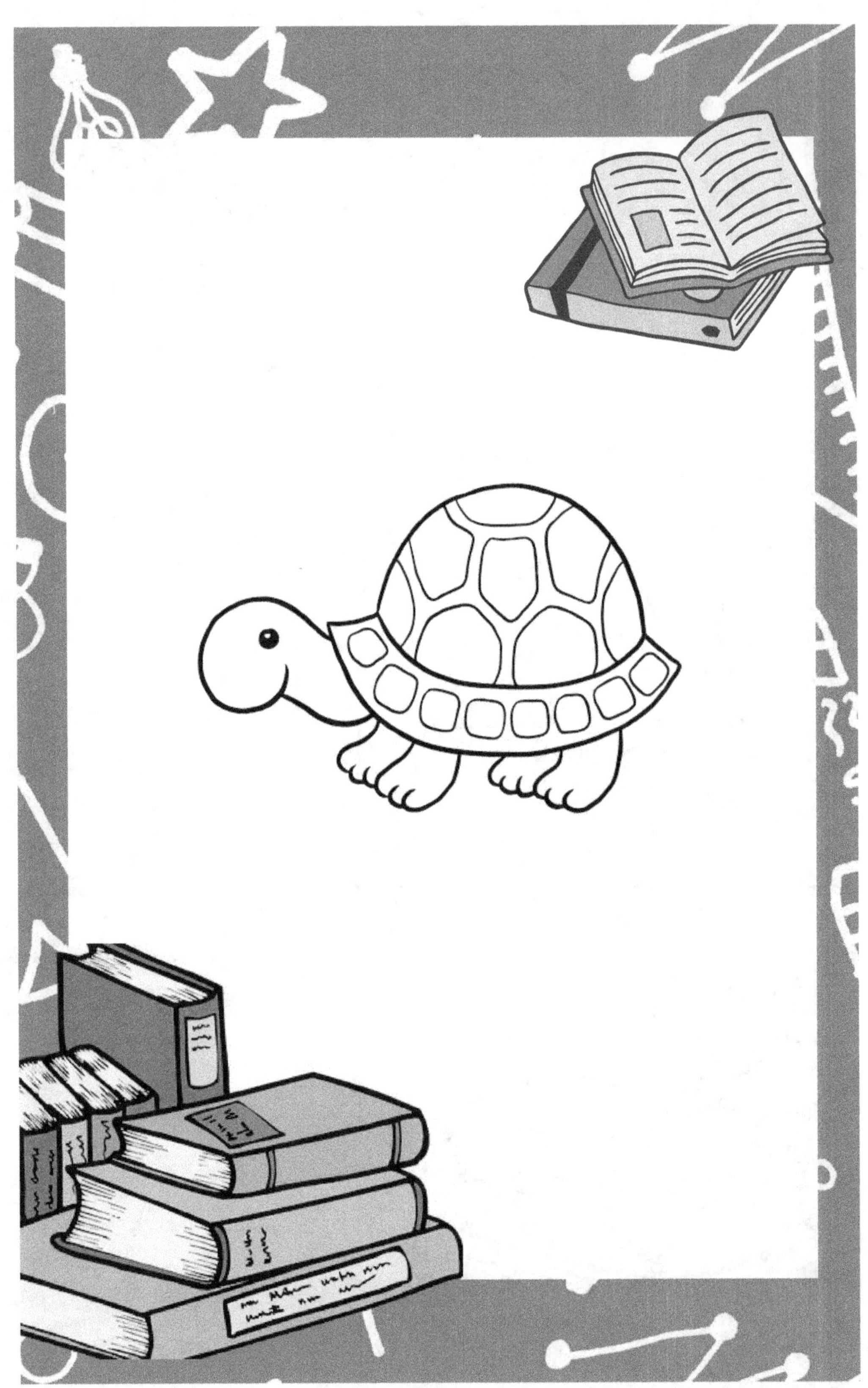

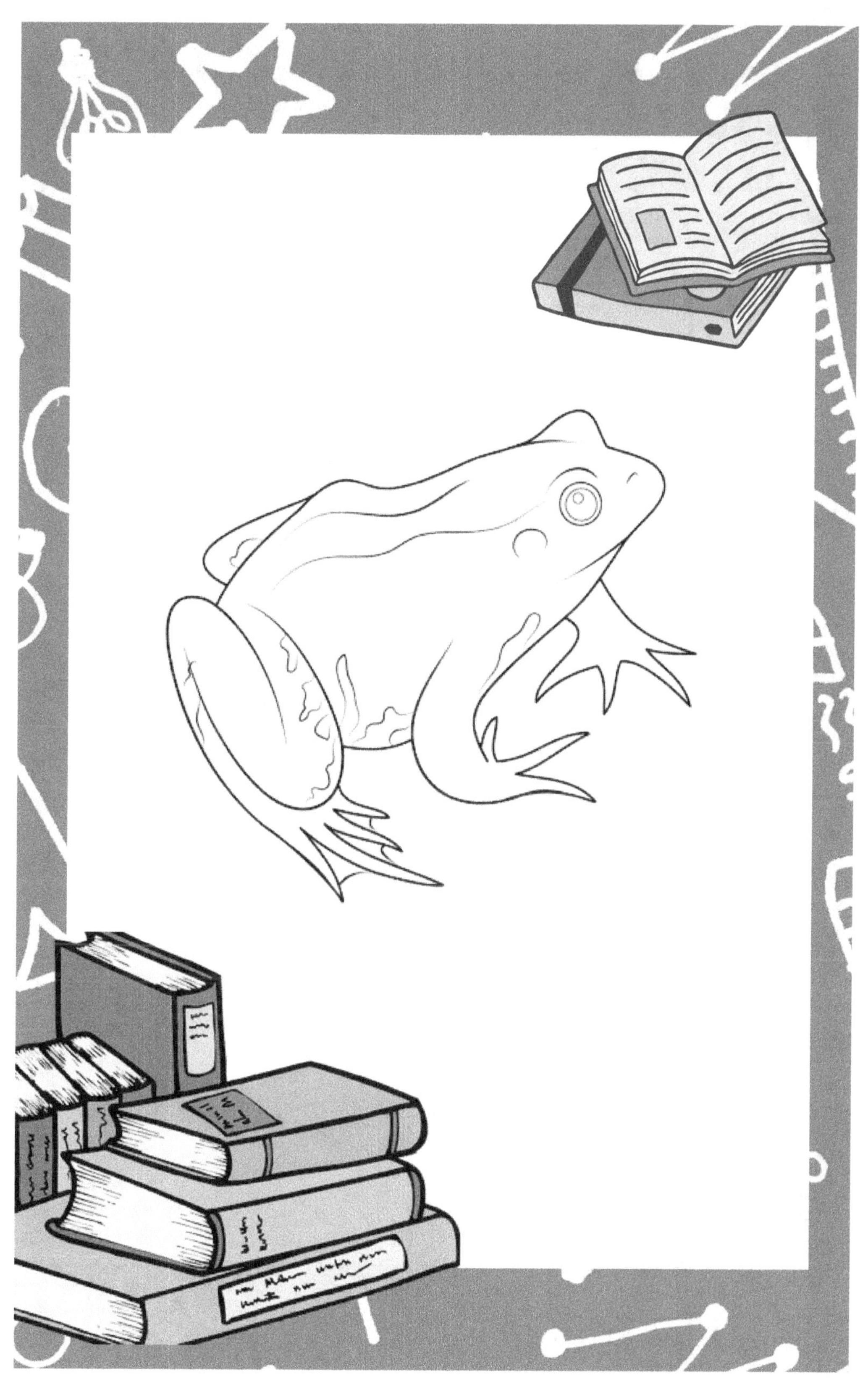

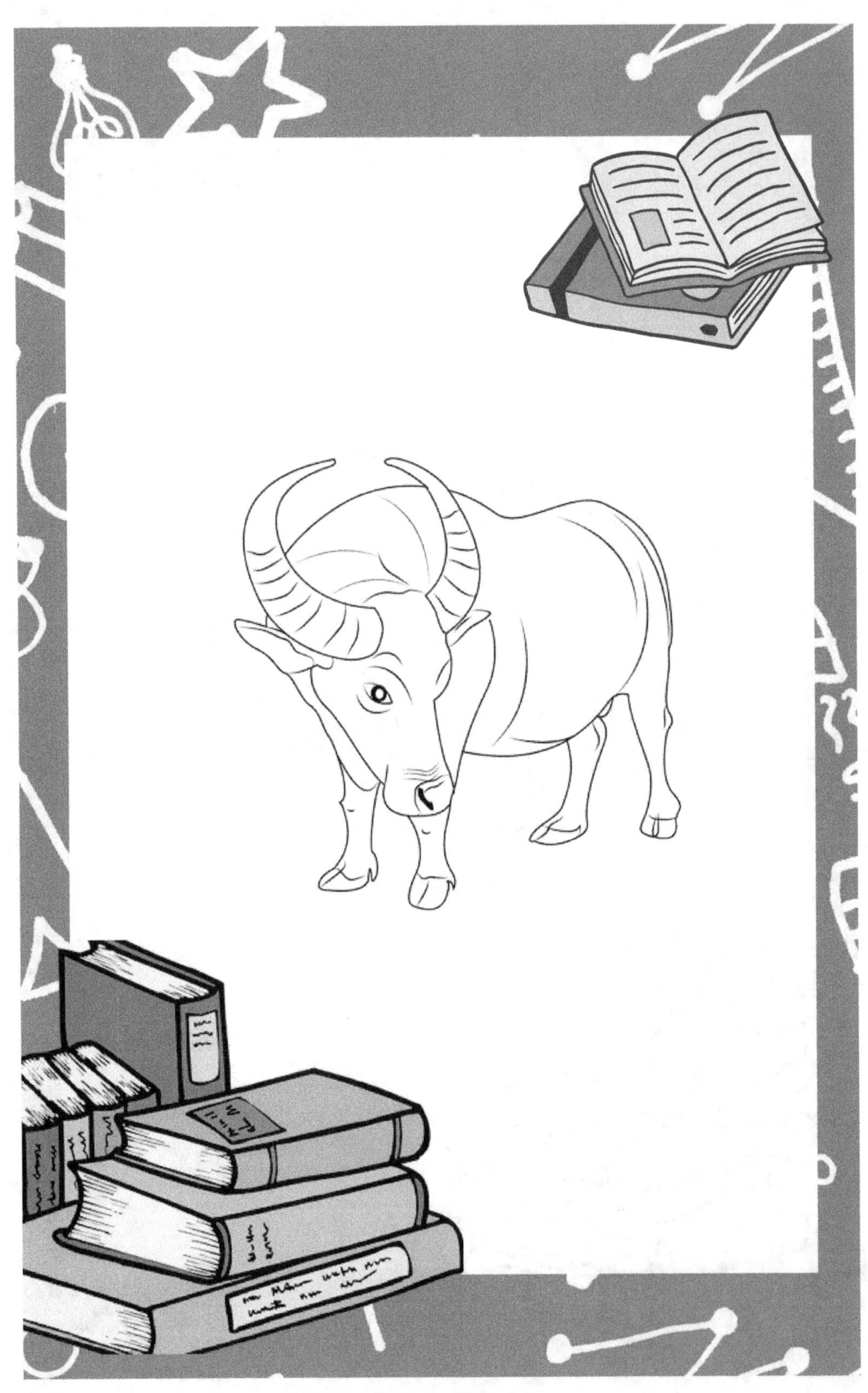

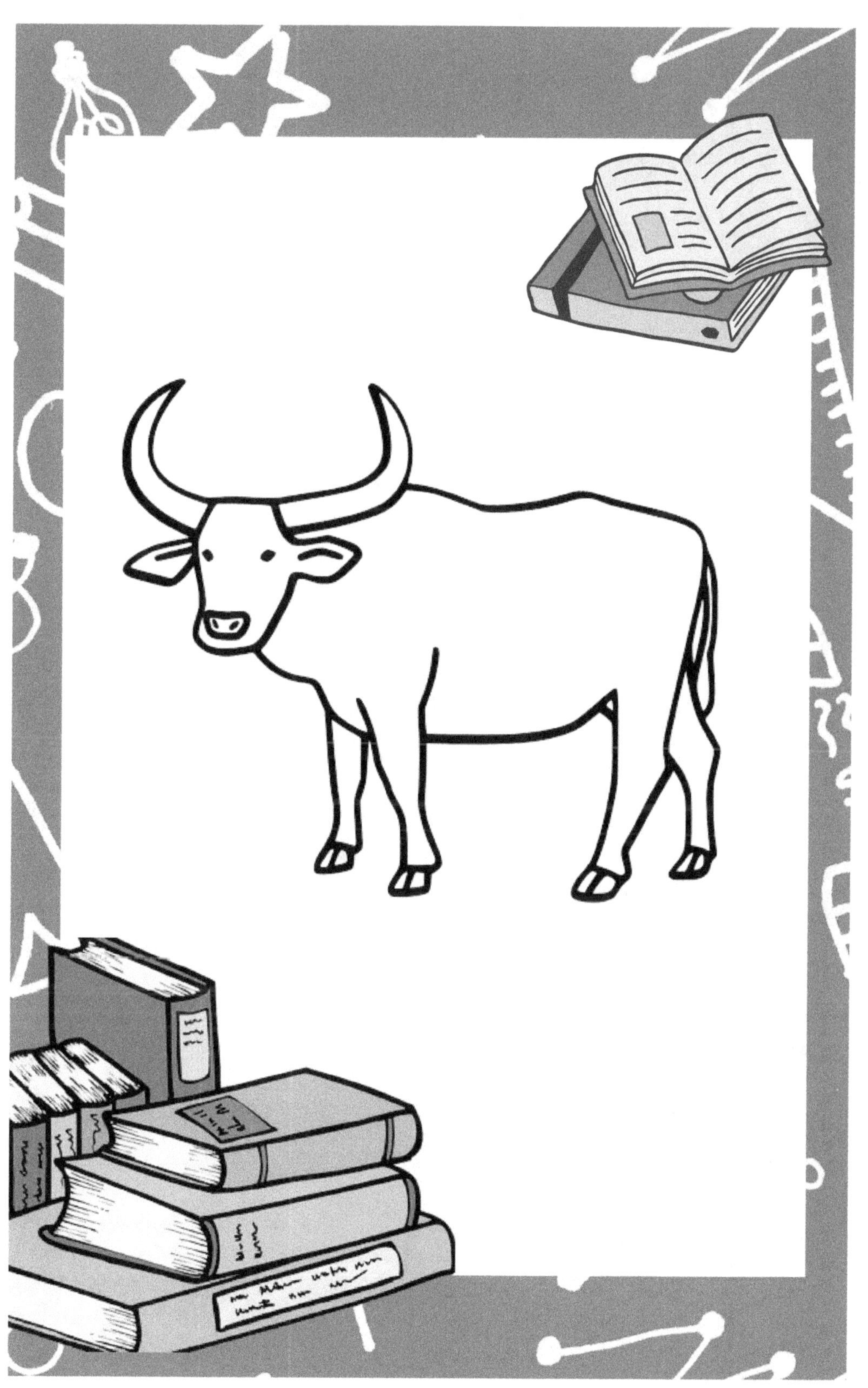

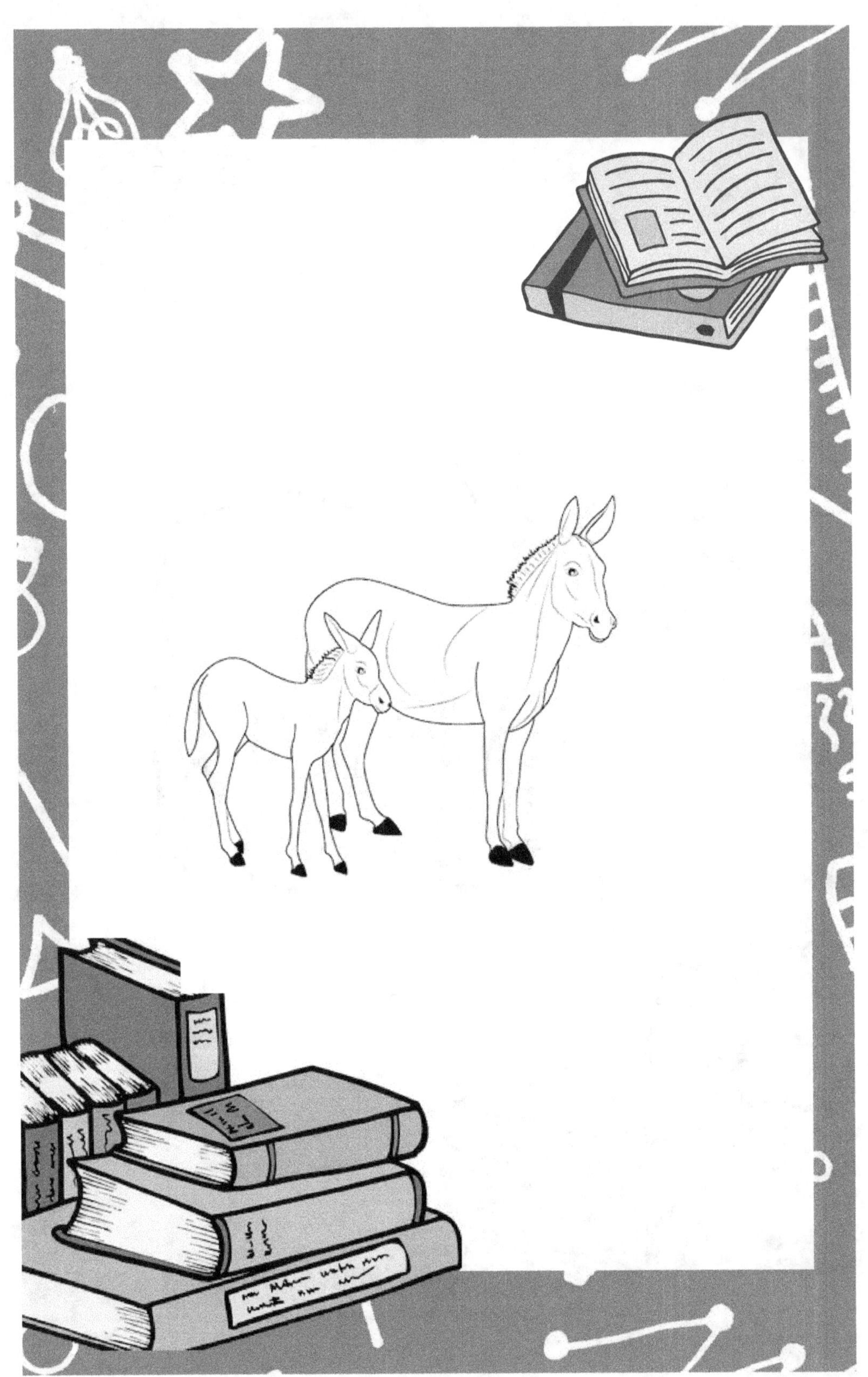

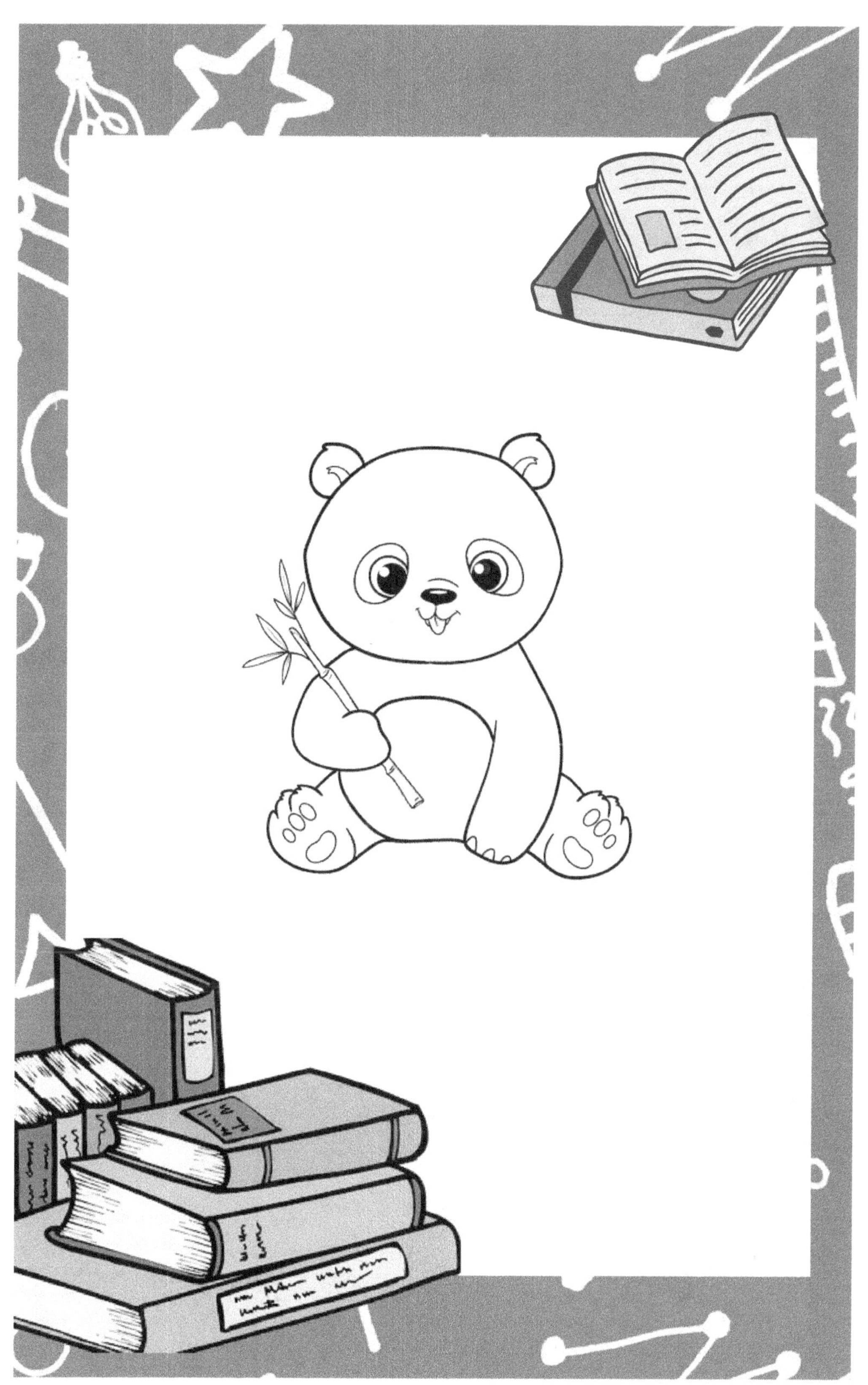

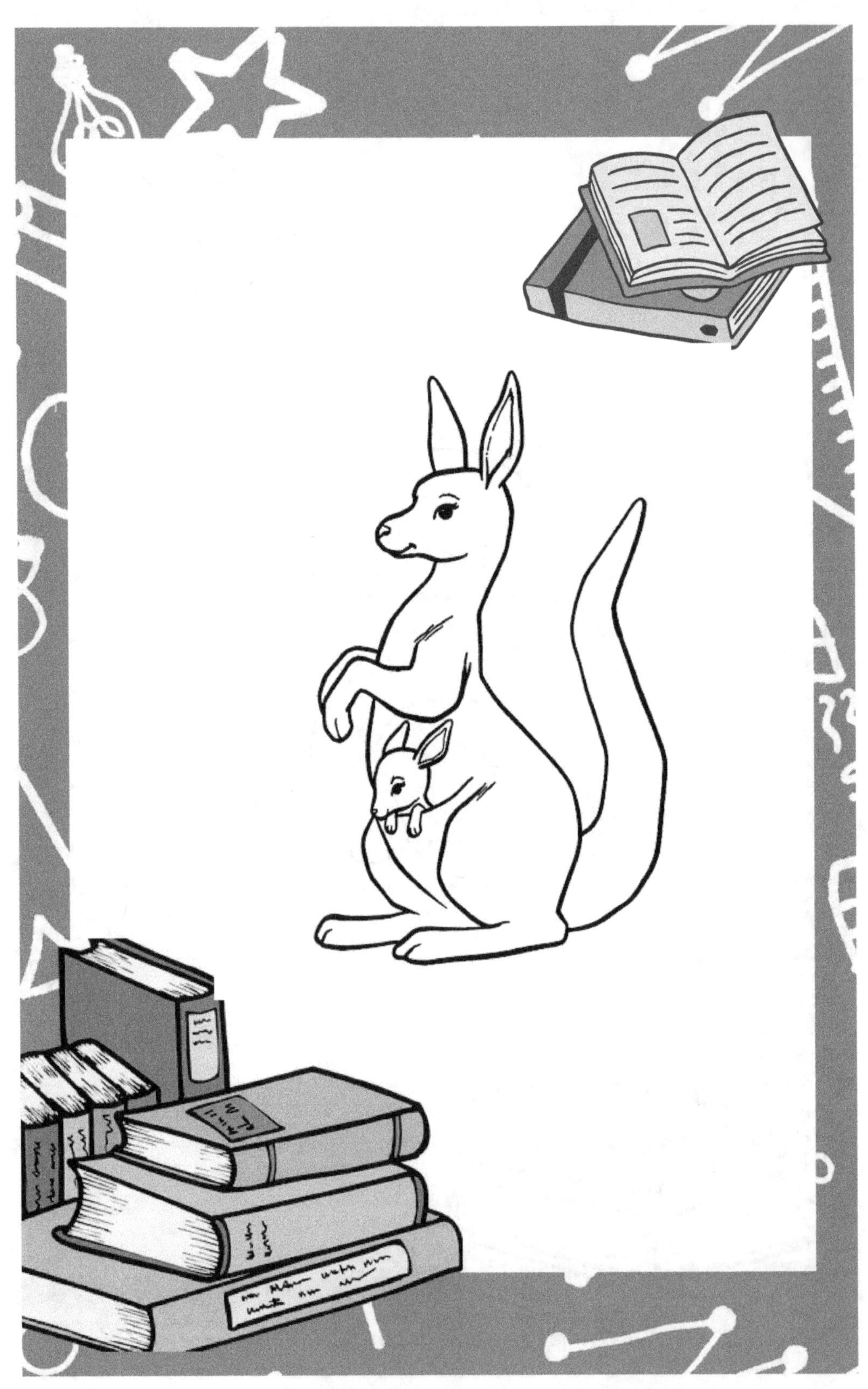

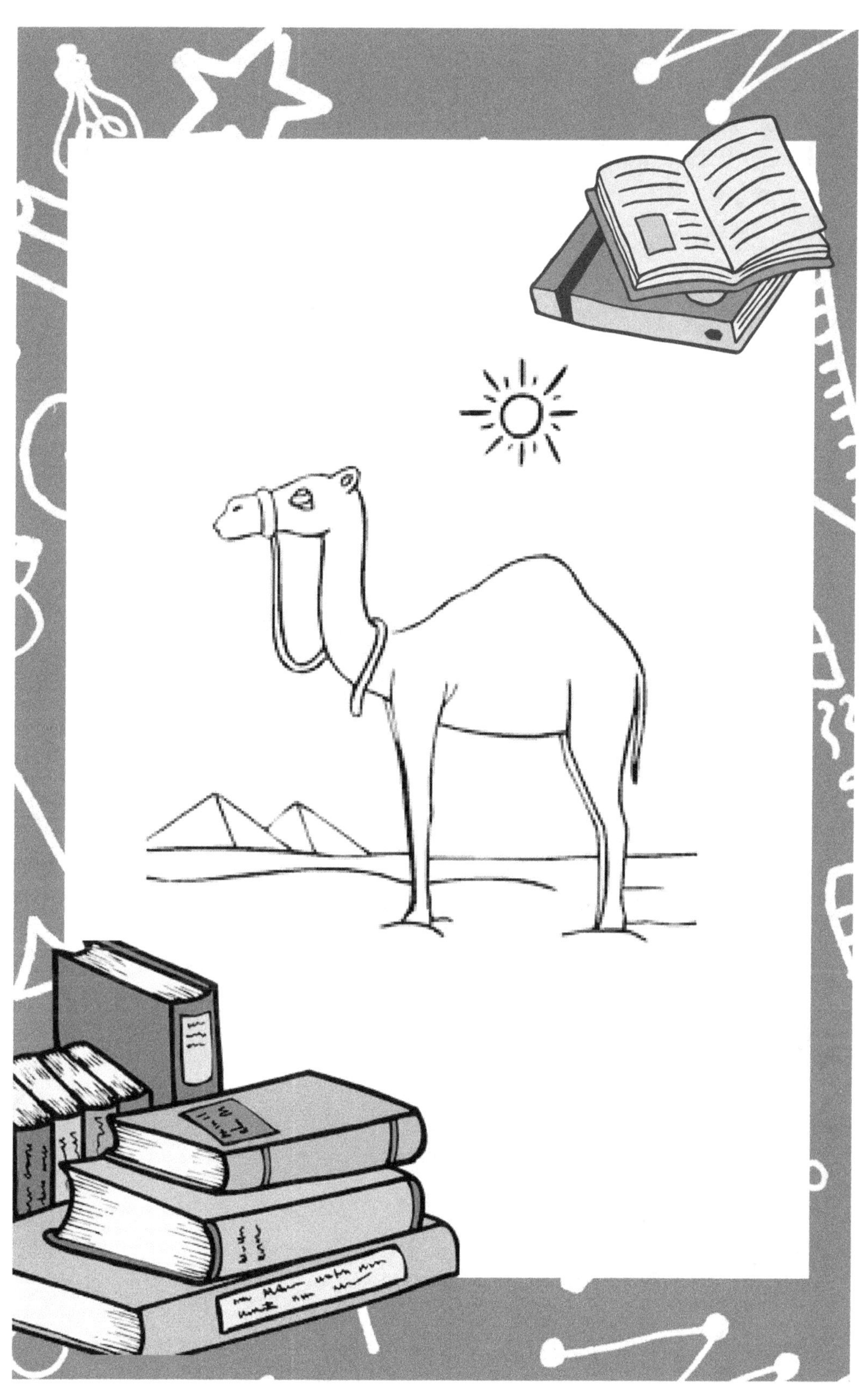

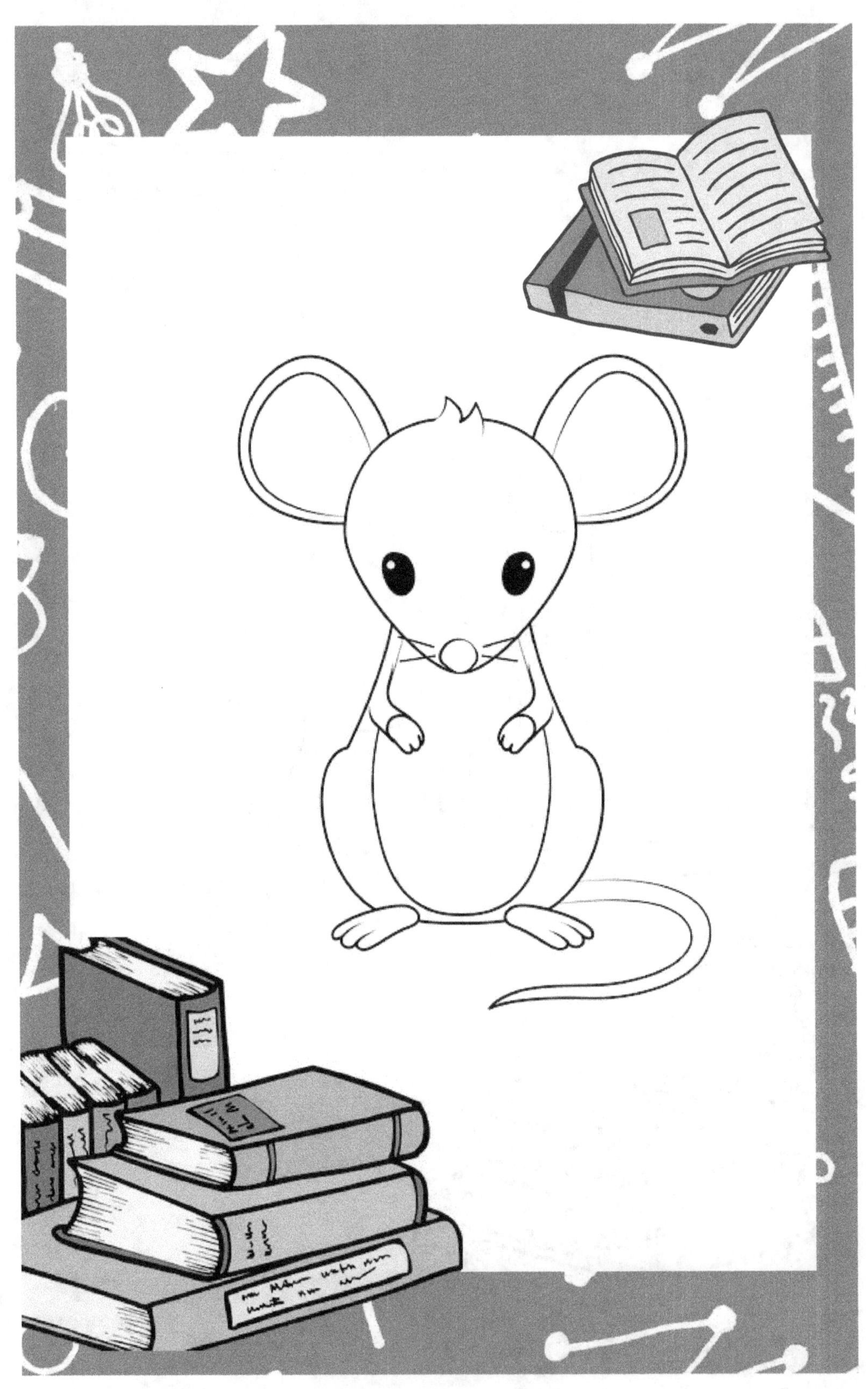

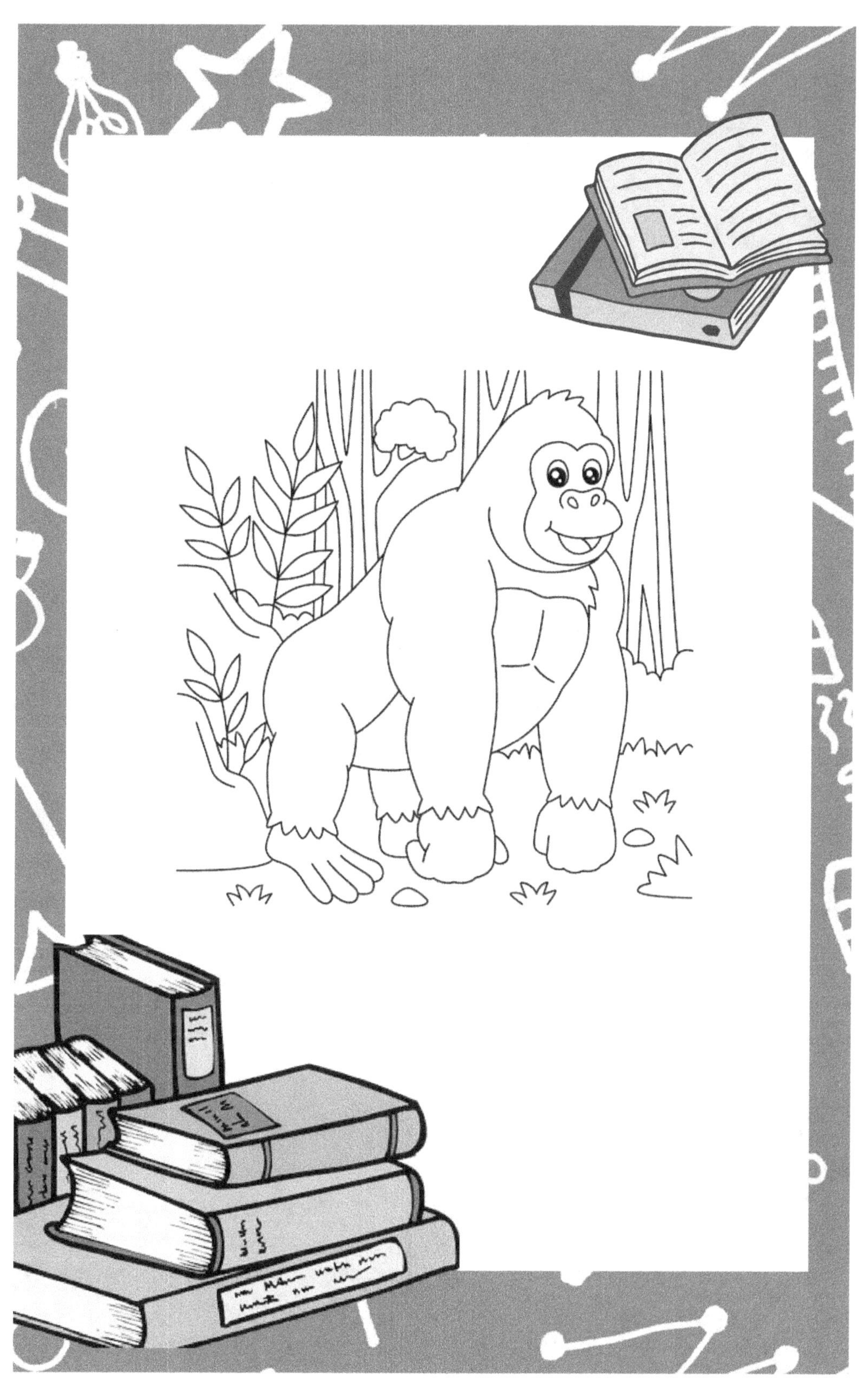

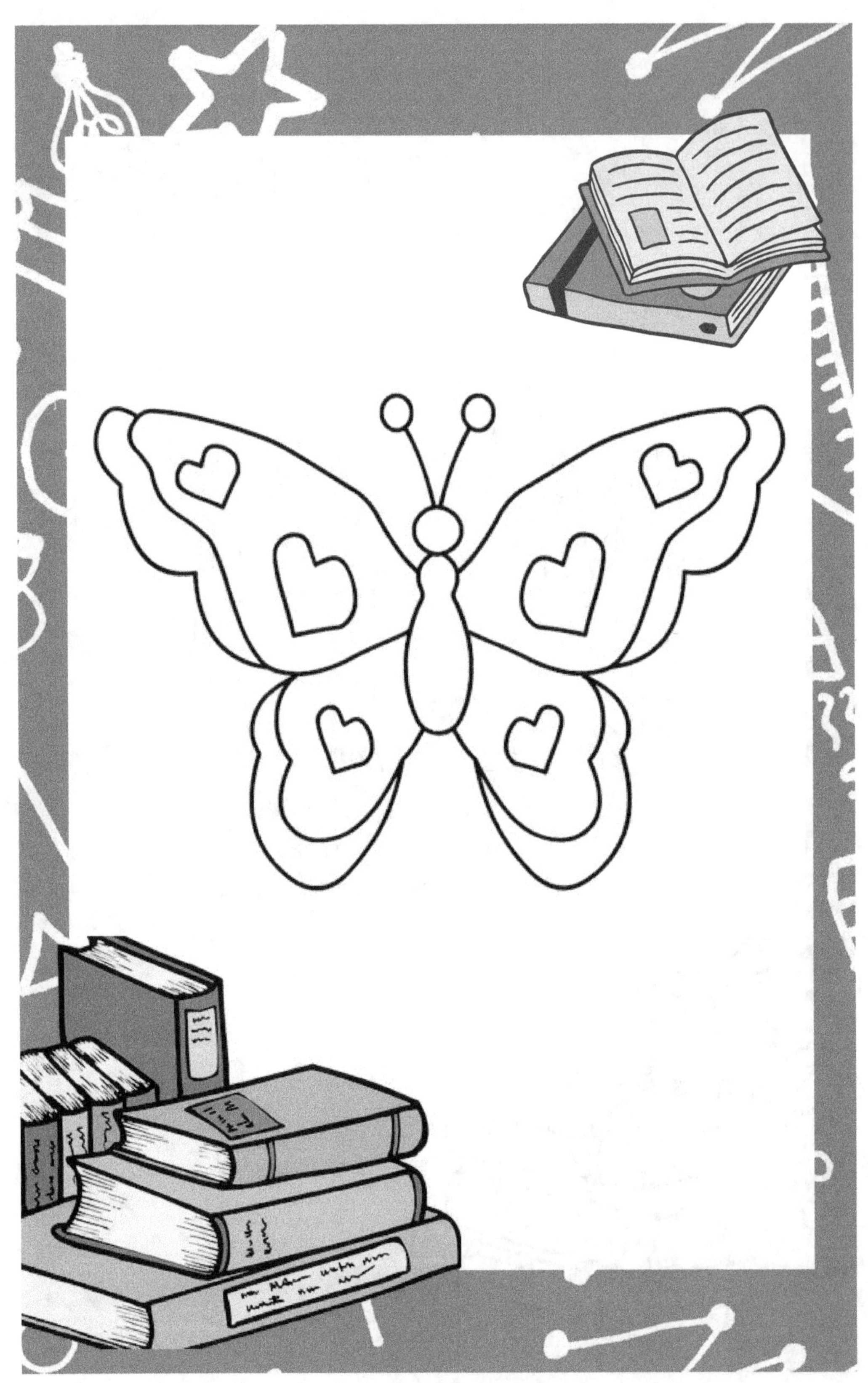

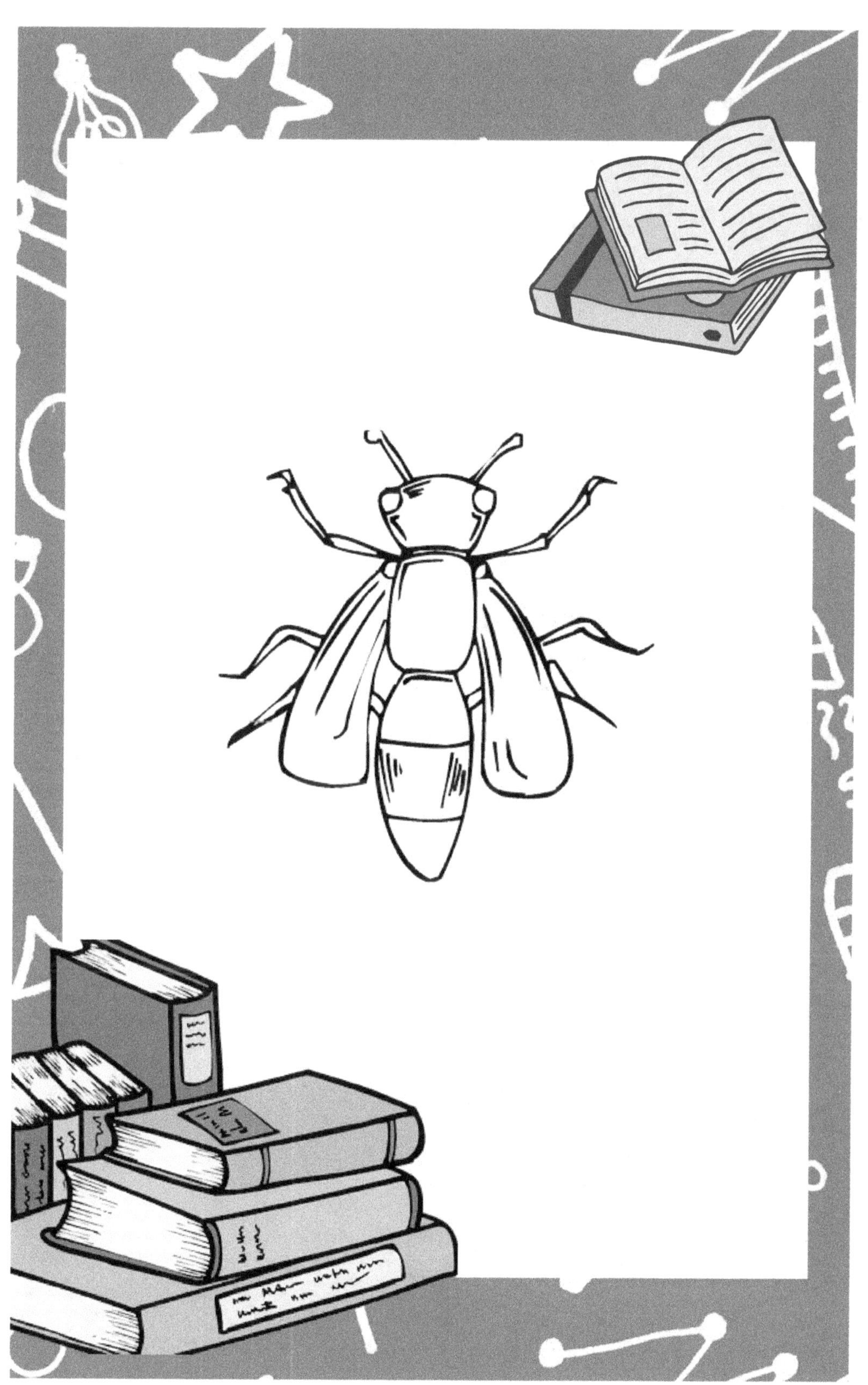

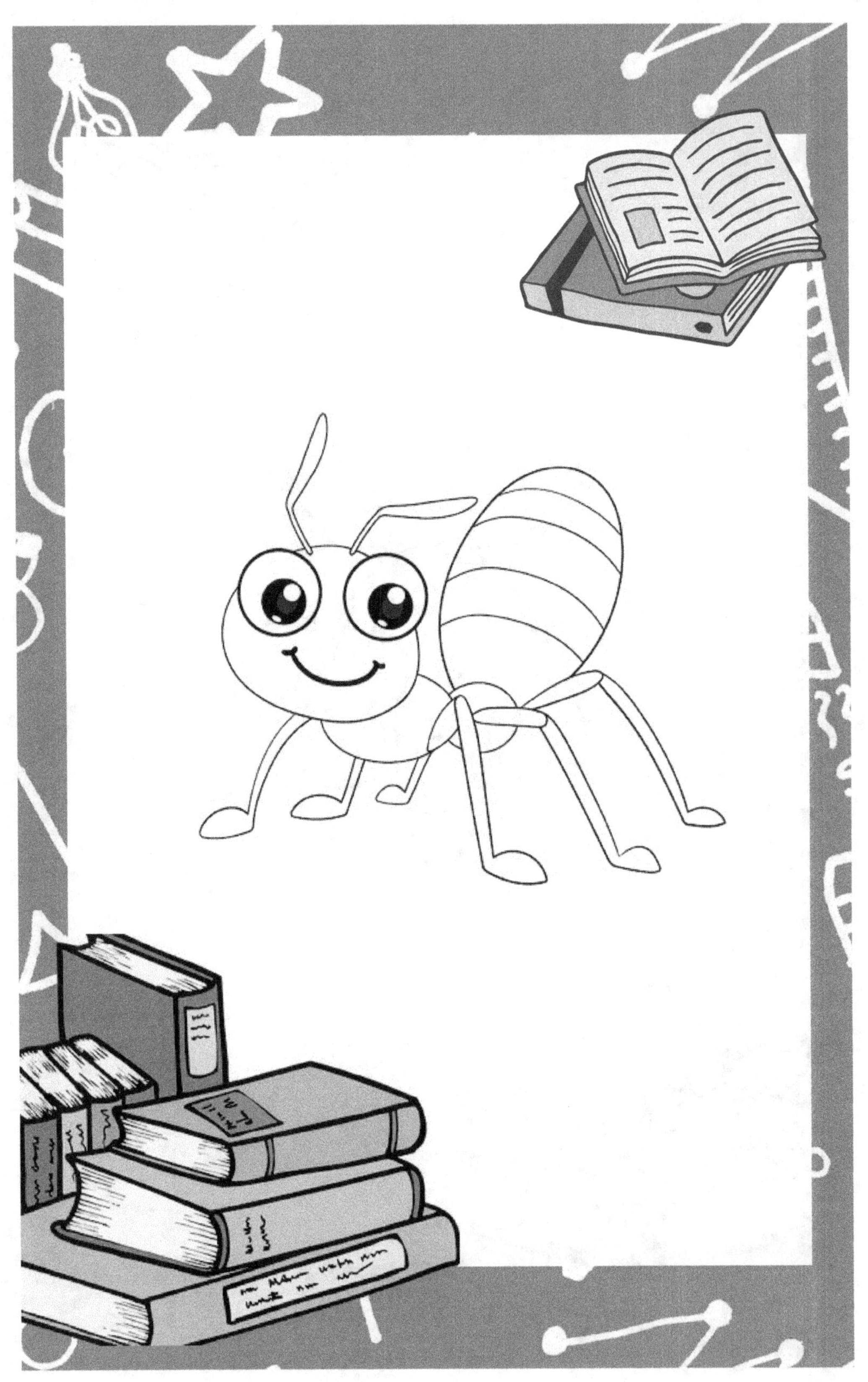